NOW HIRING!

*Finding & Keeping Good Help
for Your Entry-Wage Jobs*

Steve Lauer &
B. Jack Gebhardt

American Management Association

New York • Atlanta • Boston • Chicago • Kansas City • San Francisco • Washington, D.C.
Brussels • Mexico City • Tokyo • Toronto

This book is available at a special
discount when ordered in bulk quantities.
For information, contact Special Sales Department,
AMACOM, a division of American Management Association,
1601Broadway, New York, NY 10019.

This publication is designed to provide accurate and authoritative
information in regard to the subject matter covered. It is sold with the
understanding that the publisher is not engaged in rendering legal,
accounting, or other professional service. If legal advice or other expert
assistance is required, the services of a competent professional person
should be sought.

Library of Congress Cataloging-in-Publication Data

Lauer, Steve.
    Now hiring! : Finding & keeping good help for your entry-wage jobs
/ Steve Lauer & B. Jack Gebhardt.
        p.   cm.
    Includes bibliographical references and index.
    ISBN 0-8144-7912-X
    1. Employee selection.   I. Gebhardt, B. Jack.
HF5549.5.S38L38   1996
658.3'11—dc20   96–20824
                                                            CIP

Printing number

10   9   8   7   6   5

This book is dedicated to our children:
Wesley and **Sydney Lauer**
&
Sam and **Annalee Gebhardt**

May your bosses be always happy; may your coworkers be always congenial; and may your life's work keep you ever growing and laughing, and able to take care of your folks in their dotage.

Contents

Acknowledgments

From Steve: I would like to acknowledge my parents, Diane and Karl Lauer, who enabled me to own my first restaurant at the age of 20 by financing 80 percent of my business with over half of their life's savings. Without their faith, support, love, and confidence in me, I would not have had the wonderful opportunities of these last ten years. The older I get, the more I realize what an incredible thing my parents did for me. Thank you, Mom and Dad.

I would also like to thank my wife, who put up with my late night readings and working with this book for the past ten months, nine of which she was pregnant with our second child, and the last three weeks with a newborn daughter at home. Thank you for your support, Karen.

The following individuals were very helpful to me in completing this project: Corey Deocampo, Patti Bos, Tim Bowers, Brad Harris, and Rodger Partridge.

Last but not least, I want to acknowledge the person who got me through this book and dedicated a large portion of his time over the past year to get this project completed. I never dreamed I'd be an author, but with Jack's writing abilities and persistence, he kept me on track and moving forward. Thank you, Jack, for taking an idea for a book through my frustration with today's workforce, and turning it into a positive, helping me see the light at the end of the tunnel in this century's entry-wage workforce challenge.

From Jack: We'd like to thank the people at AMACOM, especially Mary Glenn, Jacqueline Flynn, and Mike Sivilli, for their patient and careful work on this book.

And for encouragement in this project over the short and long haul: Aneita Gebhardt, Suzy Gebhardt, Dave Adamson, Theodore Gould, John Gascoyne, and Christian Almayrac.

And to all my former employees and to all my former bosses: Thanks for teaching me your lessons! Hope you are all working twice as hard as I am!

Introduction

Where Have All the Flowers Gone?

*By working faithfully eight hours a day you may
eventually get to be a boss and work twelve hours a
day.*

—Robert Frost

Hello, Boss.

We suspect that, since you picked up this book, you are a
indeed a manager, a boss, or a business owner experiencing in
your own way the nationwide entry-wage hiring crunch. Welcome to the scramble.

We also suspect that it has come as somewhat of a surprise
to you how much more effort it takes these days just to keep
your operation fully staffed. Chances are right now you could
probably use one or two—or ten or twenty—more workers, but
that you probably have very few really viable applicants.

We suspect your classified employment ads aren't pulling
like they used to. And we suspect that when you do snag a new
recruit, you sometimes wonder what closet he's been hiding in.
Because here in the real world, he doesn't seem to know anything about working!

We suspect these things about your current employee situation because we also have recently experienced those problems.
Where have all the flowers gone? What's happening here? More
to the point, what can we do about it? This is what this book is
about.

What's Happening?

When Steve opened his first Subway Sandwich Shop in 1986, he had 150 responses to the ads he placed in local newspapers. Here, a little more than ten years later, . . . owns thirty Subway stores (life's been good!), and needs dependable help more now than ever. But a help wanted ad he placed last year in the same papers drew only five responses in a city of over 100,000. *Five responses*. Responses went from 150 to 5!

Now, Steve is not (generally) a grumpy boss, his starting pay is above average, and the hours he offers are flexible. So was he doing something wrong? Where are all the workers?

As you know, Steve's experience is not unique. Bosses, managers, and owners all across the country, in almost every industry, are complaining about the dearth of entry- and mid-level workers. More than half the shops at the new Denver International Airport were unable to stay open for their scheduled hours during Grand Opening week because, even with two years' notice, they couldn't attract enough help.

A Kmart in Ohio had to close its auto repair department for a week because it couldn't find enough help. A Circle K store in Dallas had to shut down for a week because it simply didn't have enough managers or employees to fill even half the shifts. A small video store in Boston went to self-service checkout because it couldn't attract enough employees.

When you fill up on gas, pick up your dry cleaning, or go to the hardware store, NOW HIRING signs are everywhere! Although the worker crunch is happening in every industry, the quick-serve food business has been especially hard hit. A Wendy's in Maryland was recently forced to close its evening inside service, offering only drive-up, because the manager couldn't find enough workers for both inside and out. A Burger King in Connecticut agreed to pay workers from New York City for the two-hour bus ride, each way, to entice them out of state. And besides travel pay, if workers stayed just three months with Burger King they would receive a free color television!

The stories continue: A McDonald's in South Dakota offered potential employees twenty-five dollars just to fill out an application. A chain in Milwaukee pays a $500 one-year bonus to encourage what is now considered longevity with the company. Whether the industry is food service, retail sales, "gas and go," videos, photocopies, or cleaning, solving the hiring crunch is the single biggest problem most managers face.

Causes of the Employment Crunch

Every sector of the service industry and most of the manufacturing industries are feeling the hiring pinch to one degree or another. So if you've been having problems attracting and keeping good help, you need not feel as though you're the only one rowing that boat.

Here's why we're having the problem:

1. *We simply have fewer bodies now than ten years ago.* If you had been reading the demographic reports ten years ago, you'd have seen it coming. According to the U.S. Census Bureau, the number of sixteen- to nineteen-year-olds in the population fell from 16.6 million in 1980 to 14.3 million in 1994. Since traditionally, this is the age group upon which employers have relied for entry-wage employees, the pool of hourly workers has shrunk. Many managers have been slow to recognize the need to expand their worker profile. But the dwindling supply of young workers has also had a ripple effect up through the ranks, as employers who once relied solely on young people now enter into competition for older employees.

2. *Among the fewer bodies, there is a lower desire for work.* Clearly, a smaller percentage of the young people who are available for work feel either the need or the dream for entry-level jobs. The lack of interest in these jobs stems not so much from the question of higher or lower wages as it does from a lack of social or economic motivation. They're just not applying.

Many employers bemoan this fact and ask, "What are we coming to?" We're convinced that these kids are holding back for what are actually very good reasons (see Chapter 5). As we learn to understand and overcome their boredom with working, we'll uncover a great source of energy, ready to be used.

3. *Many more businesses rely on entry-level workers than before.* Last year, the Boston Market chain hired 10,000 workers. And next year they intend to hire another 10,000. Five years ago (for all practical purposes) there was no such thing as Boston Market (or even a Boston Chicken). This is only one example of the rapid expansion in quick-service industries offering food, photocopies, gasoline, and discount merchandise—all of which are now designed to employ large numbers of entry- and middle management workers rather than trained specialists.

The Department of Labor projects that the food service industry alone will need to employ 12.5 million workers by the year 2005, up from 9.4. million in 1992. And the competitive demand for entry-level workers will not end soon. So what can you do? Just wait it out? Ignore it? Muddle on through? No. You need to move, now, with a clear and detailed plan, or you'll be like the proverbial boiled frog!

How One Frog Felt the Heat

The entry-wage hiring problem is akin to the frog in the stew pot. The story goes that if you put a frog into a pan of hot water, he's going to quickly jump right back out. But if you put him in a pan of cold water and turn the heat on low, the water will gradually warm until he's so lethargic he can't jump out. Before he comes to his senses, he's cooked!

That's what's been happening in the employment world. The heat has been rising for some years, but it's been slow and gradual. Now we're in hot water.

Steve first realized that entry-wage hiring was a problem that wasn't going away, and was not being adequately addressed, when one of his store managers, in a store only two miles from company headquarters, found himself in a position of having to hire five new workers all at once. (Steve generally has a minimum of eleven workers per store.) When the work staff gets that low, managers find themselves temporarily filling in. This manager had been filling in for more than three weeks, averaging seventy to eighty hours a week.

So the manager ran his classified ad again, and from it was able to hire enough workers to fit the schedules he had available. He gave a sigh of relief. However, within a week, four of the five workers had quit. One of them had quit before his first shift—he never even showed up. Two more left after three days. The fourth left five days after starting. Two of these workers went to higher-paying jobs, but only ten to twenty-five cents an hour higher. For part-time employees, that translates to a lousy extra five bucks a week, maximum! Had Steve known, he would have happily paid an additional ten dollars or more, just to save the hundreds of dollars in recruitment costs!

So the manager was right back where he'd started: short-handed and working overtime. Only now he had Steve's undivided attention. As a short-term solution, Steve immediately popped up the starting pay by forty cents an hour, becoming the highest entry-wage payer in the district. We learned from this that you simply *have* to be competitive with your starting pay rates—know what everybody else is paying—or you won't even be given a chance to show the good side of working for your business. Just matching the prevailing starting wage is the first ante in a poker game.

But upping the pay is only a short-term solution. The basic problem of finding and keeping good help that the manager was facing in that one store was a problem Steve was facing, to a lesser degree, in all of his stores. And it was a problem that had been growing steadily worse for several years.

Suddenly, Steve realized, "We're being boiled alive! And we are the frog plopping around in the increasingly hot water."

The People Plan

Steve realized that the entry-wage hiring crunch had become an ongoing challenge, not only to his business profitability but also to business viability. It were as if one of his major suppliers had put him on a quota and was consistently delivering only half the supplies he needed. Obviously, he couldn't just wait around for the supplier to change his polices.

So he set to work finding new suppliers, new avenues, new

ways to keep old workers longer. The results of his work are contained in this book. It's how we suggest that you, too, might view the entry-wage hiring problem.

To meet this challenge, you'll need a new type of plan, with short-range, mid-range, and long-range goals. Whereas in the past you would prepare an overall business plan, a marketing plan, and a financial plan as standard procedure, it is now necessary to also prepare a People Plan!

You need to plan where and how you'll get your new employees, what you'll do to keep them, how you will replace them, how you will promote them, and how you will inspire them. And this isn't something you can just think about whenever the occasion happens to arise, something you can do whenever it seems most comfortable. You must do it now. And as with all business plans, you'll need to establish a budget, not only for the money you'll be spending but also for the time and personnel resources your recruitment plans will require.

Goals

* Overall turnover is 25 percent or less.
* At least 33 percent of staff have a year or more tenure.
* Overall job satisfaction is prevalent, measured by pilferage, money shortage, customer response, and overall operations.
* Management turnover is 15 percent or less.

A People Plan is something you need to refine as you go along, keeping it on the front burner, because times have changed, and finding and keeping good employees is your single biggest challenge.

We're happy to report that in Steve's company, by implementing this creative yet systematic approach to hiring, his business has achieved the aggressive goals he set for himself. For the past five years he has been first in the nationwide Subway system for average volume per store for multiunit owners. He is one of the fastest-growing franchisees in one of the fastest-growing franchises in the country. Most important, he managed to keep his employee turnover rate at less than one-third the national average! This means his help wanted ads are going into the newspaper only one-third as often as those of the average entry-level employer!

Obviously, some of the best businesspeople in the country are now setting their minds to solving the entry-wage employment problem. The details on how Steve approached this problem—and how others are doing it—are what this book is all about. We have researched almost every industry that relies on entry-level workers. We've talked with business owners, shift managers, customers and, of course, the workers themselves. What we've learned and share here should quickly prove applicable to all managers struggling with this problem.

This Book Is for You

We assume you are, or could be or have been, a manager responsible for recruiting, training, and keeping hourly help. You yourself may be paid by the hour, salaried, or work on percentage; maybe you are the business owner. Although every business owner is, for better or worse, a manager, not every manager is an owner. So throughout this book we refer to managers and assume that business owners will not feel slighted. We're all in the same tug of war.

In this book you'll discover why, when you enjoy your work—and most especially the work of solving the hiring problem—you will consistently plow under, leap over, or leave behind those other managers who don't enjoy their work. And in the process of enjoying your work, you will seduce the employees of less joyful managers, enticing those workers to leave those grouchy bosses and come to work for you. And you will discover that after you've attracted new helpers, you'll (almost accidentally) also attract your competitors' customers! And, truth be told, you'll enjoy doing it. You'll enjoy the whole process. Your joy is the secret of the game.

So if you're managing hourlies right now and you don't enjoy it yet, it's time to start. This book will help you. If you're *not* enjoying yourself, this "business game" you're in is soon going to be moving too fast for you. It'll wear you down and spit you out. But when you do enjoy the game—and learning to enjoy it is quite natural and not very hard—you'll discover you're winning the game every day! You'll grow, and be nourished and rewarded by your work. And you'll help others to do the same. Enjoying your work—regardless of its nature—is the key. Since managers, as Robert Frost says, sometimes get to work twelve hours a day, it would seem prudent that we teach ourselves to enjoy these working hours!

We're convinced that a new spirit is overtaking American business, based on the idea that every worker has the right to enjoy his or her job, and this applies to entry-wage workers as well. To truly solve our hiring shortage, we must recognize this new mind-set and build upon it a new business perspective. By helping to enhance the joy of working—for yourself and those around you—you'll be tapping the power that is at the heart of every business.

Recognizing the joy of working is the basic solution to the entry-wage hiring problem. It is what puts the challenge, excitement, and fulfillment into the workday. With the guidance you'll find in this book, you, too, will solve your hiring problem and inject excitement into your own workday. It's to that end that this book is dedicated!

What the Future Holds: An Invitation

As you'll read in later chapters, the entry-level hiring crunch, for various reasons, is predicted to continue for another five to ten years. So we'd like to hear of your experiences, not only in applying the suggestions made in this book but also your own ways of dealing with the hourly-worker hiring phenomena. When you discover and share a new solution, we all are richer!

1

A Good Word About Hourlies

There is something that is much more scarce, something finer far, something rarer than ability. It is the ability to recognize ability.

—Elbert Hubbard,
American writer, printer, and editor

In the past, hourly workers have often been regarded as interchangeable, infinitely amenable, and, in a crunch, simply expendable. But the times clearly are changing.

In this book, you'll discover that we use the terms "hourly" and "hourly worker" with great affection, honor, and respect. In the same way, we speak enthusiastically of "entry-wage" workers, who most often receive an hourly wage. In some circles (professionals, salaried workers, or semi-literate business owners), these terms are still used as a subtle label of disrespect, as if an hourly worker were somehow a less valuable human being than the salaried worker or the self-employed person or the worker on commission. Some managers view hourly workers as people with less motivation, as those who will take fewer risks, and who are somehow less involved in their daily work than are workers on some "upper level." This clearly is no longer a viable view of the hourly worker, if it ever was.

"Those who don't understand what happened before they were born," said the Roman philosopher Cicero, "are destined to remain children all of their lives." So before we plunge into the future, let's take a quick glimpse back to where we've been.

That way we might have a better grasp of where we are now and where we might be going.

A Three-Minute History of the Work World

During the Great Depression, more than 2 million men and women who had previously held good positions soon found themselves out of work. For many people during that time, just putting food on the table and keeping a roof over their heads were a big challenge. So if they could get a job—any job, at any wage—the feeling was that they should take it and work hard to hold on to it. There was no sense, in the general population at least, of "do what you love, the money will follow."

Rather, people followed the money, which meant working at whatever job was offered, whatever was available. We've all heard the stories. Let's tip our hats to these valiant folks and recognize their struggles. And yet it is this still prevalent "Depression Era ethic" that keeps many managers from understanding what's happening today.

Economic circumstances change, and so do people's attitudes about work. During World War II, with so many men and women in the armed forces, and with demand high for military goods and services, many employers suddenly became short-handed. So the doors opened wide to accommodate people who had not previously been in the workforce: housewives, "foreign visitors," and young people who had recently left the farm.

Even though the workers were few and they were new to the working world, there was a spirit of working together for a larger cause—the war effort. Most workers were eager to make the effort, willing to sacrifice. And for managers, obviously the hardships of having fewer employees were slight compared to the hardships of battle. So the work ethic—get a job, work hard, hope to advance—prevailed.

In the 1950s and early 1960s, the postwar economy was booming. But the housewives, young people, and older workers, the handicapped and the new immigrants who had been filling in during the war while the soldiers were away, had all come to enjoy and depend on their regular paychecks and new opportunities. So with all the soldiers now back home, the competition for jobs was keen.

During the 1950s America saw the emergence of the "new working woman." Old taboos were falling away. It was a bright new era, a time of budding prosperity for a wide population. And everybody agreed that the ticket to prosperity was hard work, long hours, and temporary sacrifice for future gain. Most workers still had recent personal or family connections with agriculture, where a work ethic based on dawn-to-dusk farm labor was still fresh. So this was also an era of the Company Man and the Career Woman, who would willingly devote forty to sixty hours a week to the good of the company, expecting that such devotion would result in good fortune for the worker.

By the mid-1960s and into the 1970s and 1980s, the baby boomers had begun to come into the job market, and so again there soon were more people than jobs. The belief that what's good for General Motors is good for America was rapidly starting to fade. Nevertheless, employers of entry-wage workers continued to focus on their company products, their services, their systems, plugging in workers where they best served immediate business needs. ("We need a French-fry guy for the next three hours. Willie, grab a basket.") If the worker didn't like the situation, the employer just found someone who did. ("If people aren't happy in our company, we fire them!") People were on line for every job. There were applications on file and more filed every day. If truth be told, all these people looking for work were somewhat bothersome.

By the mid-1980s, demographic analysts sounded the warning: Beginning in the mid-1990s and extending to about the year 2010, the workforce is going to dwindle.

And that's exactly what's happening. The kids of the baby boomers, for the most part, are either not yet of age, ready to work, or not willing to work. And many of those kids who are both ready and willing to work—surprise, surprise—have a whole different view of what the working world is. In the last forty years of television, with the tens of thousands of roles presented, have there been more than two or three "happy heroes" who were also business owners? Or, God forbid, hourly workers? Aren't these TV sit-com roles always the antagonists, the foils, the "left-behind" people? But we get ahead of ourselves. . . .

Where Are the Warm Bodies?

With this brief history of work in America we can better understand why workers, especially at the entry level, have often been viewed simply as "warm bodies." Many employers assume it's their natural lot to have warm bodies available whenever and wherever they need them.

In the recent past, large employers of minimum-wage workers would simply give applicants the old-fashioned "mirror test." They'd hold a mirror under the applicant's nose. If it fogged—that is, if the applicant was breathing—he or she passed the test. The new employee was then plugged in wherever needed, be that the French-fry machine or the cashier's window. And if this warm body didn't work out, the employer simply fired the person and plugged in another individual.

So from the start of "scientific management" back at the turn of the century, analysts and managers have focused their efforts on such areas as controlling product quality, increasing process efficiency, gaining market share, and improving financial accountability and return. Employee management, especially at the entry level (most often minimum wage), was for the most part a matter of how many warm bodies of what type were needed where. Except for companies operating in foreign countries or in especially technical areas, the possibility of not having enough warm bodies was seldom considered, except when management had erred in its timing or underestimated its needs. In those cases, the solution was obvious and quick: run an ad, sort through the deluge of applicants, then get some more warm bodies in there to get things back to normal.

That's been the tradition. And that's exactly how most managers are still reacting to today's circumstances. But to master this worker shortage, a manager needs a much more sophisticated view of the worker. That is what this book is all about.

Why "Hourly" Is a Term of Endearment

Less than ten years ago, Steve started his career as a $3.35-an-hour "hourly." Thirty-plus years ago, Jack started his career as a 65-cents-an-hour hourly. Don't most all of us start our working lives as hourlies? To underestimate the potential of hourlies is to underestimate ourselves.

Hourly workers are the infantry of the world's economy. Hourly workers march, both figuratively and literally, with the responsibilities of daily commerce and industry on their shoulders. On payday, they get their economic rations, and maybe enjoy a little weekend R&R, but then on Monday they're back, ready to march some more. These people, paid by the hour, are responsible for defending both a company's reputation and its market share. They are the ones we send into new battlefields. We expect them to climb mountains, cross deserts, go into swamps. For us they will swat mosquitoes and suffer ants. Hourlies receive their steady paychecks, regardless of whether our business is up or down, because they work steadily.

Hourly workers show up each day and perform the tasks that need doing in order to get everybody at home fed and housed, and clothed and entertained. There's something right, something basic, something honest about hourly work. It's so basic that hourly workers constitute 89 percent of all the workers in America. If you don't like hourlies, if you don't appreciate them, then you simply don't like business. You don't appreciate the rich nourishment that private businesses provide our society through the minions of their hourly workers.

The Springboard to Advancement

Even though most of us start our careers as low-paid hourly workers, we aren't confined or limited to low-pay dead-end jobs. Hourly work generally has built into it many steps that can be climbed to move a person into higher-paying work, be it by the hour or not.

For instance, as we write this chapter, Steve is twenty-nine years old and has just come back from a three-day seminar in

Hawaii, where he talked to over 4,000 franchisees. He does such training seminars outside the normal work of running a business. He generally figures the fee for these seminars "by the hour." Last year, his seminar training revenues were, by themselves, more than double the income of the average worker in a typical state in the West. So you see, Steve sometimes still gets paid (handsomely!) by the hour.

We love hourly work! Steve is in the quick-service restaurant type of business, but what we've learned—the basics of being an hourly employee and building a business with hourly employees—the basic physics of doing this well—is the same for every industry we've studied.

We like hourlies. We love hourlies. They are our business, our sweat and blood. We were hourlies. And we suspect you have been an hourly employee (or still are one), too!

Managing Hourlies Is Not a Curse!

Let's agree right now that hiring and managing hourlies and entry-wage workers is not a curse; it's an art and a challenge that is at the very heart of a successful business. Even before you've completely mastered this art, right from the get-go, recognize that hiring and managing hourly and entry-wage workers provides you with financial rewards, as well as social, emotional, and spiritual rewards. Such rewards are the inevitable result of working happily at what you're hired to do.

Working happily? The simple truth of successful management of hourly employees is this: A consistently happy manager will consistently attract and keep happy hourly employees. That's basic physics, basic business, basic human relations. A good (happy) manager attracts and keeps good (happy) employees. A good manager is never an essentially unhappy manager.

As you'll read in Chapter 3, to be such a happy manager of hourly employees is not just a fluke. Finding happiness on the job is something every manager can (must!) do. Believe it or not, you can train yourself to consistently enjoy yourself, no matter what job you hold. And such "happiness training" is personally empowering, vocationally efficient, and just plain fun! Remember: It makes no difference how hard or easy a job is, how well paid or poorly paid, how significant or insignificant. It's what you think about the job that allows you to enjoy it.

This is the essence of management training: Good managers train themselves to think about what they enjoy about their jobs, and what they enjoy about their coworkers. Poorly trained managers let themselves think about things they don't enjoy doing. This is a simple but powerful management skill.

When you enjoy your job—when you think thoughts or tell yourself stories about your job that you enjoy—you naturally, spontaneously do a much better job than managers who don't enjoy their jobs. So one of our primary goals in this book is to give you tips, tricks, and tools to help you more enjoy your thinking about the details and all the other challenges of your job. As that happens, you'll discover that your hiring problems will spontaneously begin to dissolve, with much less effort than you ever dreamed possible.

In later chapters you will learn how to enjoy recruiting more, enjoy interviewing applicants, enjoy training new employees, and thereby enjoy attracting and keeping a full crew of happy workers. When you've learned how to naturally enjoy your job, then every day will turn out to be a good day at work! And compiling a string of good days at work is the unshakeable foundation for a successful career.

★ ★ ★ ★ ★

So, if we may be blunt, the first and best thing you can do to resolve your management problems regarding hourlies and entry-wage workers in a tight labor market is this: Quit your bellyaching! Lighten up! As paradoxical as it sounds, enjoying your problem is the quickest way to dissolve it. We'll show you how and why to do this in the pages ahead.

2

The People Plan

Consider the little mouse, how sagacious an animal it is which never entrusts its life to one hole only.
—Plautus, 254–184 B.C.

We've all experienced what happens when businesses face a worker shortage and don't have a plan already in place to deal with the problem. The first tendency is to quietly lower employee standards, back off from higher ideals—keep the poorer workers longer, hire unqualified applicants—to accommodate what is hoped is just a short-term anomaly in worker availability. In such a crunch, managers are inevitably overworked and frustrated because they find themselves stuck in this same "short-staff" loop again and again.

Knee-Jerk Reactions to the Worker Shortage

Without a plan, the knee-jerk solutions to the hiring problem generally follow this path:

1. Panic. (Yikes! We don't have enough warm bodies!)
2. Run an ad.
3. Pick up a few more warm bodies.
4. Relax a little.
5. Watch, mystified, as the warm bodies turn cold, then leave.
6. Panic again. (Yikes!)
7. Run an ad again.

And so on.

This is the path that most managers have taken at least once. Sometimes the company will take a slightly different tack. Maybe managers will put the Now Hiring! sign back in the window or ask the workers if they know somebody—anybody—else who might want a job.

It's time to put an end to these knee-jerk reactions. This book will help you, step by step, to break out of this seemingly unending loop. It is possible—even with today's worker short-age—to arrive at that happy and profitable circumstance where you have a complete, smooth-functioning staff, backed up with more applicants than you have openings for. But to arrive at that ideal future, you'll need a plan—a People Plan.

Planning is one of the basics of good business. When managers have a good plan, they have a good business. When they have a poor plan, they have a poor business. It's that simple. In Chapter 3, you'll learn how happiness is the bottom line for successful management, and you'll discover a simple four-step process for magnifying your own happiness in your daily work. Then in following chapters you'll find out how to magnify and direct your own happiness to create specific solutions to the hiring problem. This process will yield a People Plan that will ensure that your hiring needs are always met.

The Need for a People Plan

As you operate a business, most likely you have an overall business plan. You continually project what products or services you're going to offer, and where you will offer them. You visualize how your business is both different from and the same as your competitors.

Included in your overall business plan are a marketing plan, a financial plan, a plan for obtaining equipment and working space. You probably had a plan for establishing suppliers and even have a decorating plan for the decor of your new facility. For a manager or entrepreneur, detailed planning is part of the fun—and a basic necessity—of doing business.

As a business owner or manager, you are probably closely involved in planning all the little details that will make your operation function well. That's your job, and presumably your talent and your joy. The point here is that you also need to plan for your *people*—your employees.

If you haven't already, you need to develop a well-thought-out program for employee development—and then be able to implement it in a methodical manner. If your People Plan doesn't work at first, you need to play with it, change it, tinker and reengineer it until it does work. In the competitive world of business today, a People Plan is just as important—and in some instances more important—than a marketing plan or a financial plan or a plan for future growth.

The Basics of a People Plan

All of the remaining chapters of this book are designed to help you develop a way to capture and keep good people. Each chapter is one aspect of the People Plan that needs to be in place for your business to truly thrive.

The People Plan is based on three basic principles:

1. Recruit right.
2. Hire right.
3. Train right.

These principles all require planning. Although we'll discuss in later chapters the details of such planning, at this point let's review the nine essential elements that you'll have to plan for.

1. Employment Happiness

Yes, as we've said, happiness *is* something that you plan for, that you consciously monitor, steadily work with and toward, and purposely implement. As you'll discover in the next chapter, happiness in the workplace is absolutely the most important ingredient in attracting and keeping good people. With it, doing business is a snap; without it, it's impossible. So you need to plan for it every day, every week, every month. Happiness is what makes working life meaningful.

2. *Accurate Numbers*

Keeping numbers *can* be fun! And accurate numbers often mean the difference between a successful business operation and an unsuccessful one. We strongly recommend keeping reliable numbers not only on your profits and losses, and your goods in and goods out, but also on the comings and goings, the ups and downs, of your employees and of your efforts to attract and maintain reliable employees.

Following the "people numbers"—such as turnover rate, average length of stay, recruitment costs, and replacement costs—will help you treat your current staff better and attract more people, more easily, more efficiently. Numbers are "messengers of the people."

You obviously don't want to treat people like numbers. But you *can* relate to numbers as though they were people. Numbers will talk to you, play with you, hide from you, surprise you, teach you, and befriend you. By the way, if you're a manager and haven't yet learned to enjoy your numbers, you may have a "false ceiling"—something that will put a halt to your career and that needs to be removed. Until you do learn to enjoy the numbers, you probably won't rise very far in the business world. In Chapter 4, we'll show you how.

3. *Your Employment Needs*

This sounds so easy: "I just need another cashier," or "I need a good stock clerk." But defining what *kind of* cashier or what *kind of* stock clerk you need goes a long way toward fulfilling the second principle of the People Plan: Hire right!

Some managers are so panicked at being short-handed that they simply hire the next living, breathing warm body who asks for an application. Other managers carefully plan, define, and know precisely who they're looking for in a new employee. Most managers are somewhere in-between.

Knowing ahead of time who you're looking for makes your work much, much easier. Prepare a job description. Write down the job skills, personality traits, hours available, social skills, and work ethic that you would most love to have in your new employee. When you have this new employee clear in your mind, you'll be giving the universe a better opportunity to fulfill your expectations. See Chapter 5 for a fun view of today's new workforce!

4. Recruitment Strategies

Once you know *who* it is you want to come to work for you, you are better able to plan *where* you are going to go "fishing," and what you're going to use for bait, when the best time is for trawling, and so on.

When it comes to recruiting, it's wise to have a backup plan. And it doesn't hurt to have a backup to the backup either, just as it's wise to take more than one hook or lure with you when you go fishing. When you have a sale, you don't just put out a single flyer. You generally use banners, newspapers, balloons, a sign on the street, signs inside, buttons for your people, and so on. So, too, with your recruitment plan. You need more than one dimension. There's a lot more information on recruitment strategies in Chapters 7 and 8.

5. Interview and Hiring Techniques

The interview is where you close the deal. You surely don't want to plan for everything else but then neglect to plan for the close! You need to plan an interview that is as informative for your prospective employee as it is for you. You should make the whole process enjoyable, easy, leading to the natural conclusion of the new applicant's wanting to come to work for you.

We suggest writing scripts for these interviews, planning the setting, and having backup support to help woo the new employee. Is this unusual? Yes. Is it now necessary? Yes again. It's a win-win situation. Put some thought into the close of your interview and see the other ideas presented in Chapter 9.

6. Tools and Training

You need to plan on how you're going to supply your employees with the proper tools and the training to use those tools. And then you need to plan on how you'll give them permission, as well as the time and space, to learn and experiment with these tools—to come to know the tools so intimately, and use them so expertly, that they consider themselves "true professionals" in their work, be that at the cash register, the gas pump, or the computer scanner.

We're talking here about both physical and metaphysical tools. For instance, it's not enough to have a high-quality mop and an $85 mop bucket. It's also necessary to have first-hand experience and a conscious understanding of why we all work better in a clean environment. Your employees deserve high-quality equipment and even higher-quality training on that equipment. Without it, they'll be looking around for something that they feel is more deserving of their time and talents. We cover the subject of training in Chapter 10.

7. Employee Retention

You need to plan on what you are willing to do to retain your employees for a long period of time. We put great emphasis on retention of employees because it is one of the two or three basic keys to solving today's hiring problems.

The theory is simple: If your employees don't quit, you don't have to hire new ones! As we write this, 41 percent of Steve's employees have been with him for one year or more. This is two times better than the national average for quick-service restaurants!

The secret to retaining employees is to make your workplace a fun, clean, profitable, ethical, and adventurous environment. If you say this doesn't sound like "business," then you've missed the point of what the future is going to be all about! Tomorrow's business is going to be about all of these things and more, not only for workers but also (thank God!) for managers and owners. We trust that every chapter in this book will help you, one way or another, to better retain your employees. We discuss employee retention more pointedly, however, in Chapter 11.

8. *Communication and Motivation*

You have to plan to communicate and motivate. These two absolutely critical managerial skills go hand in hand, and can be accomplished at almost no costs with just a little bit of time, patience, understanding, and awareness.

The best things in life are free and in the world of management this old saw holds true again. By simply giving your employees their rightful, honest, human, positive strokes on a daily basis you can turn your average employee into a happy, hardworking long-term worker. For some managers, offering these simple human expressions of appreciation, kindness, and positive reinforcement takes work. If you as a manager can't find two or three things your employee has done well on the shift he/she just completed (or completed the night or day before), then you better either reconsider his or her employment or your own! Generally employees will perform at least ten duties correctly before they do one incorrectly. However, that one incorrect action is the one we as managers usually feel most inclined to discuss! Imagine what the response would be if you called your employee at home to say, "I just wanted to call and let you know how great the place looks this morning after you closed last night."

Planning to communicate and motivate works! And it makes a positive difference in everybody's day! This has been proven time and again. It does take some time and conscious effort until you make it a habit. But this is a habit that your staff will be glad you developed! In the next chapter on "Planning for Happiness" you'll see more clearly how to do this.

9. *Positive Public Image*

Everybody likes to work for an upscale company that has a good reputation in the community. It's easier to get good help if you have a good reputation.

A large part of having such a good reputation comes from having earned it through good business practices, good hiring practices, good firing practices, and high-quality products and services to the community. An important part of that good community reputation, however, comes through good public relations that was planned and orchestrated to let the public know about those great products and services, as well as those humane business practices.

For instance, over the years Steve's company has hired thousands of people within the communities in which he does business. He can't help wondering what his ex-employees are saying about him to their families and friends. Do the spouses, parents, and children of his employees and ex-employees have good impressions of him? From such reports, will some of these friends and family members be willing to respond to his employment advertisements?

Every aspect of recruiting, hiring, training, retaining, and firing or saying good-bye to employees is an aspect of public relations—the business's public image. A good name in the community goes a long way toward helping ease your hiring problem. You need to have a plan to keep this reputation intact, including exit interviews and worst-case scenarios. A plan for creating a good public image is more than just a plan to do good business. Time and money need to be allocated to make sure the news gets out, when and where it should, about the quality of life at your company. Chapters 11 and 13 will help your business maintain a good public persona.

★　★　★　★　★

We recognize that these elements of the People Plan are not new in this age. They have always functioned at the heart of good business. However, the current work environment doesn't allow managers to just "get by" dealing with two or three of these planning elements. Today's managers need to do all nine of them in order to compete in the fast-paced, competitive arena. A wider and wider circle of managers and business owners is coming to the necessity of these elements. We plan our businesses with them in mind. So this is the competition you are facing in your business.

As you continue reading this book, you'll discover ways to

implement your own People Plan that will carry your business through the next decade. But first, let's look at the most basic and powerful of all elements necessary to attract and keep good people: happiness. You'll be happy to discover that achieving this element is really very simple.

3

Planning for Happiness

Genius is the ability to simplify those things we perceive as complicated.

—C. W. Gran

Work should be more fun than fun.
—Noel Coward

A book that has had a major influence on our understanding of successful personnel management is *The Customer Comes 2nd*, by Hal Rosenbluth and Dianne McFerrin Peters. Rosenbluth took over his family's travel business when it had annual revenues of $20 million. Over the next fifteen years he built the business, with what some might consider contrarian management philosophies, into the largest travel business in the world, with yearly revenues of $5 billion. And what does Rosenbluth say is the key to his company's success? "There is nothing we believe in more strongly," he says, "than the importance of happiness in the workplace."

The title of his book, *The Customer Comes 2nd*, comes from the idea that the worker is the "horse" of every business and the customer—whom the worker is there to serve—is the "cart." To put the customer first and the employee second—the traditional notion of corporate management—is like putting the cart before the horse. Rosenbluth puts it this way:

> To serve our clients best, we have to put our own people first.
> The principle . . . is straightforward. It's our people who pro-

vide service to our clients. The highest achievable level of service comes from the heart. So the company that reaches its people's (employees') hearts will provide the very best service. It's the nicest thing we could possibly do for our clients. They have come to learn that by being second, they come out ahead.

We agree with Rosenbluth that to ensure the best service for your customers, you, as a manager, must take into account your own employees' happiness. We take this idea one logical step further, however, and suggest that it is your happiness that is the single most important ingredient for ensuring your employees' happiness! Fortunately, when it comes to happiness, it's not an either-or situation. In fact, the happier you, as manager, are with your job, the happier your employees are, and thus the happier your customers will be.

Dr. Christian Almayrac, a French physician, international lecturer, and powerful management consultant, has articulated four very simple principles, which in their entirety he calls the BeHappy™ Game. These principles provide a step-by-step approach to achieving happiness in the workplace. After you are introduced to these four steps, you will discover that you have, to a certain extent, already been playing this game in your own work situation . As Dr. Almayrac says of these principles, "What I say out loud, you already know in your heart."

This is a "life game." The most successful people—not only in business but in every field of endeavor from ditch digging and homemaking to ministering and brain surgery—follow these principles, use these steps, and play this game at one level or another. You will find, however, that when you follow these four principles and make the game a daily tool to work with, then you will immediately and dramatically increase your ability to enjoy your daily work experience, and thus will be more successful.

When the steps in the game are written out like this, on the surface they appear quite simple and obvious, but they are seldom recognized as the core of management or business life. Nevertheless, they are, indeed, the essence of every successful management practice.

Step 1. The Law of Happiness

Your enjoyment of your work is the most important thing for you and for all those around you.

For most managers, understanding the importance of enjoyment is generally a no-brainer. When presented like this, the truth is obvious and apparent. Wouldn't you, either as a boss or an employee, rather work with someone who enjoys his work? So in either position, the most important thing you can do is to enjoy your work!

When you hear such simple wisdom, it rings true deep inside. But how often do you let it guide your day? As a manager, you obviously have many different levels of important work that you must accomplish in order for the wheels to keep turning. It's important to have your schedule, and important to have all your raw ingredients—your inventory, your basic goods— available for your workers, and available on time. And it's important to have all your time cards appropriately filled out, and your withholding forms filled in. These things are important because it's necessary for you as a manager to help turn a profit for the business. It's important to watch costs. It's important to please your boss. And it's important to please your customers. It's important to have the right number of people with the right training in the right place at the right time. We know there's a whole truckload of "important" things for you to do. The importance of all your managerial duties is not disputed.

The key, however, and the point that is so often overlooked, is that *the most important* thing is for you to enjoy your work. If you, as a manager, are doing something you inwardly do not enjoy, you and everybody else will feel it.

And in such a case, whether it's your boss, your employees, or your customers, other people's experiences in relating to you are likely to be at least somewhat unpleasant. Thus, you're *not* helping the business, and when you are not helping the business, you're not doing your most important managerial job!

During the rush of the day, it may often seem that the details of business are more important than your own sense of happiness. But they're not. The point of the Law of Happiness is that these details are of secondary importance to the inner joy that you as a manager must consistently feel doing your job.

For instance, if, without losing your inner sense of joy, you can talk to one of your staff about the importance of being on time or having the salad fixings in the right bin or not taking too long a break, then you are worth a hundred times more than the manager who talks to her staff about the exact same things but doesn't enjoy herself while she's doing it. If you stay with your joy, your staff will not feel threatened, will honestly listen, and will honestly respond! When you are happy, you are more efficient and you engender more loyalty.

No, this is *not* a lesson that came out of the Depression. This is a lesson born of today. The manager who enjoys her work will attract and keep good people. The manager who doesn't, won't. It's as simple as that.

So, how do you as the manager remain connected with your inner joy? You learn about the Law of Linkage.

Step 2. The Law of Linkage

You enjoy your work when you enjoy the thoughts you are thinking and the stories you are telling right now.

The Law of Linkage gets its name from the fact that it links happiness with your thinking process.

Again, when so simply written out, as it is right here, it's a no-brainer. It's obvious, clear. As Dr. Almayrac tells his audiences, "I have never been able to enjoy myself when I think thoughts I do not enjoy. And I have never met anybody else who could enjoy themselves while thinking a thought they did not enjoy." Yet to think thoughts about your work that you do not enjoy seems to be a cultural tradition—one that's changing, thank goodness! So to enjoy your work is actually a very simple matter. It doesn't have anything to do with your boss, your schedule, your responsibilities, your coworkers, your history, or your customers. It has to do with what you choose to think. Simply choosing to think only the thoughts and stories about your work that you enjoy thinking about, whether these are positive, negative, or neutral, will keep you energized, on top. Radical as that may sound, that's all it takes!

But again, tradition and cultural heritage so often steam-roll this simple key to a happy working life. We will allow ourselves to be happy, we tell ourselves, when:

* Our pay is better.
* Our coworkers are more helpful.
* They fire Jerry the Jerk.
* We get promoted.
* They give us the respect we deserve.
* They change the dress code.
* They change our hours.
* We're given credit for all we've done.

And on and on and on. As William Shakespeare had Hamlet say 300 years ago, "There's nothing either good or bad, but thinking makes it so." Charles Swindoll, the best-selling motivational author also writes, "I am convinced that a happy life is 10 percent what happens to me and 90 percent how I react to it."

Happiness in your work is always, 100 percent of the time, within your power. It depends not on your circumstances but on how you react to and think about them.

You need not play the BeHappy Game perfectly right from the start, any more than a golfer is required to consistently hit a hole in one or a bowler is expected to bowl perfect strikes, one right after the other. But by using these four steps—remembering them, practicing them—you begin training yourself and expanding your ability to remain in your state of happiness much more than you ever would have believed possible for someone immersed in the hectic fray of daily business.

So how do you begin training yourself to enjoy all of your thoughts about your work, all of your stories, all of the time? First, by asking this simple question: "Am I enjoying myself?" This takes us to the Law of Spontaneity.

Step 3. The Law of Spontaneity

Whenever necessary, ask yourself, "Am I enjoying this thought about my work, yes or no?" If the answer is not an immediate and spontaneous yes, then it's a no.

Since, as we've agreed, enjoying your work is the most important thing for you and for everybody else, and you can't enjoy your work unless you are thinking thoughts that you enjoy, then you deserve to be absolutely certain that you are indeed enjoying yourself. You don't want to have to guess or hem and haw about whether you are enjoying your work or not. By requiring an immediate and spontaneous yes to the question, "Am I enjoying myself?" there is never any doubt.

It's as if you are selling shoes in a shoe store. Shoes are your basic product and so important to your welfare that you never want to run out. So when a customer comes in and asks if you have any shoes, you would never say "Well, it depends on what you mean by a shoe." You want to be absolutely clear, absolutely certain. "Yes, we have shoes, big shoes, little shoes, fat shoes, skinny shoes. What kind of shoes do you want?" It's the same thing with your joy, with your happiness on the job. You deserve an immediate and spontaneous answer.

"You do not need to define happiness to know what it is," says Almayrac. "You may not have a definition, but if I ask you if you are enjoying the thought or the story you are thinking right now, you can answer, right away, yes or no. If it's not an immediate and spontaneous yes, it's a no. I have worked with many thousands of people, and I have never once had someone tell me they did not know when they were enjoying themselves and when they were not."

In other words, you don't need a definition of happiness before you can be happy! The simple, ordinary happy feelings you have about yourself, your coworkers, and your job are the real goods! As Almayrac notes, it's like when you ask your lover if she loves you. If she asks, "What do you mean by love?" you know you're in trouble. You don't want there to be any question. You want an easy, immediate, and spontaneous yes.

Ok, but what if you are *not* enjoying yourself, your job, and your coworkers all the time? Then what? What can you do about it? That's explained with the Law of Joyous Action.

Step 4. The Law of Joyous Action

If you are not enjoying your thoughts about your work (i.e., if you're not enjoying your work), you have two options:

1. *You simply choose to enjoy that same thought that a moment before you were NOT enjoying; or*
2. *You drop that thought that you were not enjoying and choose a thought that you enjoy more.*

This is called the Law of Joyous Action because it requires that you do something with your thoughts. If you are not enjoying your job, this is the action to take! In other words, choosing your thoughts—and choosing to enjoy your thoughts—is how you remain happy in your job! First, you manage thoughts.

Basically what you are doing when you apply both the third and fourth principles—the Law of Spontaneity and the Law of Joyous Action—is taking control of your thoughts. Or at least assuming responsibility for your thoughts.

If it is your job to take charge, to take responsibility, doesn't it make sense that the first thing to take charge of, the first thing to take responsibility for, is your own thinking process? Once you begin managing your own thoughts—choosing only thoughts that you enjoy—you'll be surprised at how easy the rest of your work becomes.

Keeping the thought: The story of Pat Griffin is an example of the first option—of allowing yourself to enjoy a thought that only a moment before you didn't enjoy.

Pat Griffin, the inventor of the first coin-operated gas pump, and originator of the first self-service gas station, was a young man working in an old-fashioned gas station, pumping gas, when he thought to himself, "What am I doing here? It doesn't take any skill to pump gas. Anybody could be doing this. Anybody could be doing what I'm doing."

"Anybody could be doing this" was a thought that Pat Griffin at first did not enjoy. He felt he was stuck in a low-paying, low-prestige, unskilled job. And then, in the next moment, he allowed himself to enjoy the exact same thought: Anybody could pump his own gas!

At one moment he didn't enjoy the thought. The next moment he did. Same thought, different approach. And thus he invented the self-service gas pump. The difference between joy and no joy was a multimillion-dollar difference!

The difference between enjoying our thoughts and not enjoying our thoughts is *always* a profitable difference, even though it may not be a multimillion-dollar difference. Try it, you'll see!

Changing the thought: Almost every child will naturally, spontaneously offer a clear example of the second option. As a child, especially a very young child, if there were thoughts you didn't enjoy thinking, you were naturally adept at simply and quickly dropping those thoughts and thinking thoughts you enjoyed more.

As the screen door slammed behind you, on your way out to play, you spontaneously dropped all the thoughts you didn't enjoy. The same thing happens when adults get involved in a favorite pastime such as watching football or going shopping. In both instances we allow ourselves to drop the thoughts we don't enjoy. We don't figure out how to enjoy a football game or a shopping spree. We just drop the thoughts we don't enjoy thinking, and go about doing, thinking what we enjoy more! Can we let our work be even "more fun than fun" as Noel Coward said it should be?

Some worried managers might suggest that it's irresponsible to just drop thoughts you don't enjoy. In fact, however, that is the most responsible thing you can do, for yourself and for everybody else!

Clara Sue, already ten minutes late for her shift, calls in and says she can't find a baby-sitter, so she won't make it in today. It's the third time this month. As the manager it's your responsibility to either start calling around and find someone to take her place or break the news to the others that they'll be working short-handed.

You don't feel like being gleeful and happy-go-lucky, and you don't have to be. But you also don't have to be bummed out. You're going to have to deal with Clara Sue sooner or later, but you can't right now because she's not here. So rather than be mad and grumpy and upset as you call around, you put Clara Sue out of your mind—you drop the thoughts you aren't happy to think—and think thoughts you are happy to think: Billy Bob might enjoy a few extra hours, or Francis, living alone, doesn't mind coming in at all, or Winthrop is maybe just sitting home doing nothing anyway.

"Hey, Billy Bob, Clara Sue just dumped on me again and I'm looking for someone to take her shift. I'd be happy if you could come in, won't hold it against you if you can't. What's happening in your world? Feel like making some extra dough, and making a friend of your manager for life?"

You don't need to sugarcoat reality just to enjoy yourself in every situation. You also don't need to carry Clara Sue, and her problems, with you for one more minute than is absolutely necessary!

In order to make work more fun than fun, as Noel Coward suggests, you must be brave enough, strong enough to drop all the thoughts you don't enjoy about it. When you are so brave, so strong, then your work will be more efficient, more successful, more easily accomplished.

If you simply can't find any thoughts at all that you enjoy about your work, then perhaps it's time to enjoy thoughts about changing your job! But this is always a dangerous suggestion because, nine times out of ten, if you can't enjoy where you're at, you haven't trained yourself yet to be able to enjoy where you're going! But there's no law saying you have to practice your happiness in one place as opposed to another. The only allegiance you owe is to your own happiness! If you'd rather enjoy yourself in a different job, do it! You, your old company, and your new company will all be better off for it.

When the scriptures say, "Come unto me as a little child," the implication is to come to exalted consciousness through thoughts of joy and peace and wonder. Remember, a thought is just a feeling. And a feeling is just a thought. Louise L. Hay, author of the multimillion best-seller, *Heal Your Life,* says, "A feeling is just a thought that is moving through the body."

If you want to change your feelings, change your thoughts. It's not a long-term process, it's an immediate action, like watching a football game. You're feeling gloomy because the home team is losing and suddenly they intercept a pass and you're feeling great! If you are feeling bad right now, it's because you are thinking something you don't enjoy right now. Intercept that thought—take it the other way!

Who Is Happy and Why?

David G. Myers, a social psychologist, conducted one of the most exhaustive surveys ever on the topic of who is happy and why. He reported his findings in his book, *The Pursuit of Happiness.*

From his extensive research, Myers isolated four primary traits of a happy person. (By the way, he concluded that, on the one hand, it was impossible to tell if somebody was faking happiness. And on the other hand, it didn't make any difference, because those who were faking happiness seemed to enjoy the same benefits as those who were in fact happy! Point being, even if you are not happy, you can fake it, and before you know it you're thinking thoughts you actually do enjoy thinking!)

The Four Inner Traits of a Happy Person (Manager)

1. *Self-esteem: Happy people (happy managers) like themselves.* Self-esteem is not a mysterious, ephemeral quality given by grace only to those who happened to have a perfect childhood with perfect parents who have grown up to acquire perfect occupations.

The mechanics of self-esteem are in fact quite simple: When you think thoughts you don't enjoy about yourself, and your work, you diminish your self-esteem and your work. When you think thoughts you do enjoy about yourself and your work, you enhance your self-esteem and your working conditions. It's all within your control.

Enhanced self-esteem is an automatic result of practicing thinking about what you most enjoy thinking. That's one of the beautiful results of playing the BeHappy Game. You'll discover that by practicing this game that the four traits of happy people automatically arise.

2. *Personal control: Happy people (happy managers) believe they control their destinies.* As we move into a new century and a new millennium, it is more and more apparent to more and more people that the world we live in is determined by the thoughts we think. Although this truth is just now coming into popular awareness and greater acceptance, it's not a new principle. Henry David Thoreau said, "You fail in your thought, or you prevail in your thought alone." And Thoreau, writing more than 100 years ago, was encapsulating the wisdom of the centuries.

As you learn—through the BeHappy Game—to control your own thoughts, with the gentle guidance of joy, you more and more control your own destiny. And, one thought at a time, you ensure that your destiny is one of joy and delight. Every destiny—every tomorrow—is built on the foundation of today. You can not create a joyous tomorrow if you are unhappy today. Only by being happy today—practicing happiness today—can you build a foundation for a completely full and happy life!

3. *Optimism: Happy people (happy managers) are hope-filled.* When you are hopeful, you are thinking thoughts you enjoy. When you are in despair, you are thinking thoughts you don't enjoy. Again, the BeHappy Game brings you naturally, easily, to express all of the traits of a happy person.

4. *Extroversion: Happy people (happy managers) are outgoing.* Undoubtedly, there are effective, efficient, highly productive introverted managers. But they are in the minority. As Mickey Spillane said, "The race doesn't always go to the swiftest. But if you're a betting man, that's where you put your money." The manager with an outgoing personality is likely to be more effective than one who is withdrawn. But again, it's not just a matter

of fate—whether you were given an outgoing or a withdrawing personality.

As you enjoy your thoughts more, you naturally, spontaneously, enjoy both your surroundings and other people more. When you enjoy your thoughts, you aren't as inclined to hold them in. When you enjoy your thoughts, you are happy to share them. As Mark Twain noted, despair grows in solitude; happiness grows when it's shared.

Practicing the BeHappy Game, you gain confidence and self-esteem. And with confidence and self-esteem, the outgoing personality is more likely. We are not talking here about the boisterous, glad-handed salesperson who dominates every room and conversation. Such social aggressiveness is often an attempt to make up for self-doubts and a lack of perceived inner worth.

An easy, natural, flowing friendliness, on the other hand, comes from long practice of thinking what you most enjoy thinking, about yourself, about others, about your job, and about the world.

So here we've covered the basic requirement for attracting and keeping good help. No matter what you learn through the rest of the book, if you're not naturally enjoying your job, if you're not consciously practicing the BeHappy Game, or some form thereof, then no matter how clever your help wanted ads, or how intriguing your training programs, or how good your pay scale—if you're not enjoying yourself, and enjoying the process, you'll not succeed. For joy, itself, is the mark of success. When it's present, you're successful. When it's not present, you're not successful.

★ ★ ★ ★ ★

With this foundation, we can now move into the details of attracting and keeping happy hourly employees and entry-wage workers.

4
Happy Numbers

A Three Sentence Course On Business Management: You read a book from the beginning to the end. You run a business the opposite way. You start with the end, and then you do everything you must to reach it.

—Harold Geneen, C.E.O./I.T.T., from *Managing*

If you don't know where you're at, it's close to impossible to figure out where next you should go, let alone what you'll need to do to get there. In this chapter, we'll be encouraging you to set up numerical systems to track the particular nature of your unique hiring conditions.

The Need for Numbers

As we mentioned in Chapter 2, the three basic ingredients for dissolving the hiring crunch are recruiting right, hiring right, and training right. So how do you know when you are doing these things right?

The first clue is that you begin enjoying recruiting, hiring, and training more than you've ever enjoyed these activities before. Your joy is the sign that you are doing something right.

Your second clue is numbers. Your numbers tell you when you're going forward and when you're going backward. Unlike joy, which is immediate, your numbers must be accumulated over time. And speaking of time, when Steve was a youngster, he was crazy about playing baseball. If he could have, he would have played baseball every day, all day, seven days a week. He played it for fun; he played it for companionship; he played it to improve his skills. He was—and still is—baseball crazy.

He generally played shortstop and was pretty good at it—good enough to be captain of most of the teams he played on. Like a lot of guys, he was dreaming about playing college ball and then maybe. . . .

Alas, his collision with the left fielder and center fielder simultaneously smashed his knee and brought an end to his baseball fantasies. It was his first and most painful experience with "poor communication."

As a kid, Steve had started tracking his numbers—his hits, runs, errors, times at bat, consecutive innings of play, etc.—from when he was nine or ten years old, which was when he began his earliest organized youth league games.

A lot of the other kids thought he was crazy for keeping such close tabs on his numbers. But to Steve, it was just another dimension of the game which he could also enjoy. And by paying attention to his numbers, being aware of where he stood and how he was doing, his skills improved more rapidly and came under his control more readily than was true for his neighborhood pals who just played the game and then forgot it. The numbers allowed Steve to be more focused. He knew his strengths and his weaknesses. He knew where, when, and how he was either helping or hurting his team.

Now, as a business owner and manager of over 350 employees, Steve still enjoys playing the games by watching the numbers. We hope to convince you that you too can enjoy tracking and watching the numbers, which is a dimension of the game that will always help you improve and is essential if you are ever to maybe "make it to the majors."

Here's another example. Jerry Gilles, well-known motivational speaker and author of *Moneylove*, tells a story about a factory owner who was frustrated by the presence of a bowling alley located across the street from his factory. The factory owner would often find many of his employees shirking their duties and slipping across the street to roll a heavy ball at some distant pins, an activity which he himself gauged as much more boring and repetitive than the "real life" game he was offering in his business. He called in a management consultant to help him meet the problem.

"What would happen," the consultant asked, after studying the situation, "if you put a sheet across the front of the pins, so that the bowler couldn't tell how many pins he'd knocked down, and so couldn't track his accumulated score?"

"I suppose he'd lose interest pretty fast," the factory owner said.

"It's the same with their jobs," the consultant said. "If they have no way of knowing where they're at, or where they're going, or how well they are doing, or if they don't know whether they are hitting or missing their target, they lose interest real fast."

This principle—know where you're at, know where you're going, know whether you are hitting or missing your target—is a basic concept that applies to all aspects of business, even the seemingly simple chore of digging a ditch. The ditch digger wants to know—needs to know—how deep, how wide, and in which direction he should dig. In the same way, your employees want to know the "standard" for their work.

You as a manager need to have specific standards for all the different areas of your own responsibility. If such standards are not clear, and aren't tracked, both you and your employees will soon lose interest in the process and fail to hit the targets. Doesn't it make sense that the same principle holds true for catching, training, and keeping happy hourlies? Sure it does. You need to track your hiring and firing, your employees' coming and going by the numbers! The first thing to do is establish—by the numbers—a budget for your hiring process.

Important Budget Numbers

It's possible to fly by the seat of your pants when it comes to hiring, training, giving time off, or doubling up on hours. As a manager and business owner, there are times and even whole seasons when you want to ditch your plans and your budgets, and just fly by the seat of your pants, managing by "gut reaction." Such an approach to business is sometimes necessary, even advisable. But long-term success and daily peace of mind require a more studied, more numerical approach. To begin, you need to have at least a rough idea of what your labor costs are, expressed either as a percentage of sales or a straight dollar figure for the week, month, or quarter. Labor costs should include all costs associated with the recruiting, hiring, motivating, and keeping of employees.

Every business is different when it comes to appropriate labor costs, but once you have at least a rough idea, then you need to budget those costs to cover these five areas. Not everybody has time or energy to budget, but you need to at least *track* these areas so you know where you can improve.

1. *Recruiting.* How much time and money do you spend finding "new blood"? You have to consider the costs of running your classified ads, making and dispersing flyers, creating new ideas, and paying "sign-up bonuses" or up-front incentives. You can just throw time and money at the problem, or you can work out a numerical budget, a plan.

2. *Hiring and training.* How much time and money are you spending on interviewing, orientation, training, and everything else it takes to get a new employee through the starting gates? Again, are you flying by the seat of the pants or are you establishing a budget and staying with it?

3. *Beginning and continuing wages.* Your starting wages are what will get new employees to walk through your door, so that you can woo them further. How much do you have to budget to get them through the door? This generally does not depend on your own business but rather on the work climate in the town or city of your business. You need to compete, but you don't necessarily want to put all of your labor costs into one basket. If you do, you'll have people coming in the front door and going right out the back door! You need to keep a little in reserve in order to retain your new people.

4. *Motivation costs.* You may have planned on offering "crew incentives" or trading out products and services, or costs of donuts or pizzas or movie passes, as ways of keeping employees. These are the little "perks" that make working for your com-

pany a little easier, a little softer, more humane. You need to include these seemingly spontaneous "extras" in your budget, however, to keep your employees moving and grooving.

5. *Retention bonuses.* Keeping your crew happy day by day, week by week, will improve your retention rates. Nevertheless, it always pays to offer, from the beginning, a financial reward for longevity. A company should offer perks and special rewards for "one year and over" employees, such that every employee quickly recognizes the benefits of hanging in there for the long haul. Long-term employees are the most valuable employees you have. Isn't this obvious? Doesn't it make sense to put more eggs into this basket? But you must budget for these costs!

When you have budgets set up for each of these areas, you'll be able to gauge how you are doing, where you're spending more than expected (or necessary), and where you're not spending enough. Without a budget, you're flying by the seat of your pants, and the employee turnover maelstrom is going to spin you in circles. Having these costs itemized and in place will help resolve your hiring problems for the least expense.

Now let's look at where else you need numbers to help your business fly.

Tracking the Turnover Rate

We often give talks and conduct seminars with business owners and managers around the country, and we're always astounded to discover that as many as 75 percent of these owners and managers don't know what their employee turnover rate is! When asked for a show of hands, many of them don't even know what a turnover rate is!

Your *turnover rate* is the annual rate—expressed in a percentage—at which you "turn over" your working crew. That is, it is the percentage of people you have to replace every year. A rate of 100 percent means that you must hire one whole new crew each year. Many managers, even when they are aware of their turnover rate, often express it in vague terms, saying, "it's pretty high," or "it's pretty low," or "about average, I'd guess."

We believe that a business's turnover rate is directly related to its bottom line. Thus, to say "it's pretty high" or "about average" is like saying, "I don't know what my income was this year, but I'd guess it was about average." These are important numbers that you need to know exactly!

Why track your business's turnover rate? The turnover rate is a key "flag" for how the business is doing. In Steve's company, when he suddenly sees an unusually high turnover rate in a particular store, or when a turnover rate in a particular store just starts gradually creeping up, then he knows that the individual manager is having some kind of problem.

For example, it could be that the area of the city where the store is located is changing demographically, or there's new competition in the neighborhood, or even that someone else on the crew is creating discord. More often than not, however, a rising turnover rate indicates that the manager, for one reason or another, has lost her spark and thus is losing employees. Tracking your turnover rate helps flag and quantify these personnel challenges early on, before they become too costly.

With the hiring crunch as it exists right now, you can be sure that in five years' time every top manager will know and track his turnover rate, as surely as every top bowler knows and tracks his bowling average or a ditch digger knows how deep and wide he's supposed to be digging.

The turnover rate is a numerical sign of the health and vitality of a business, as surely as the numbers associated with profit and loss, labor costs, and retained earnings! For a People Plan, the turnover rate is one of the prime numbers used to monitor the success of your entire operation.

In a growing number of businesses dealing with today's hiring crunch, a portion of each of the manager's quarterly bonus is based on turnover rate. Each of Steve's managers knows her turnover rate, expressed as a numerical percentage, and works hard to hit the company targets that have been set for her. Here's the basic formula for calculating your turnover rate:

$$\text{Turnover rate} = \frac{\text{number of replacements}}{\text{average number of employees}} \times 100\%$$

For instance, if you hired fifteen different people during the year, and the average number of people in your shop was ten, then your turnover rate would be 15 percent.

In the quick-service food industry, the average national turnover rate is approximately 300 percent. This means that a business must replace all its workers three times a year. Steve's turnover rate for the last five years averaged 140 percent, less than half the national average. For the full-service restaurant industry the national turnover rate averages between 125 and 150 percent.

Turnover rates for different industries vary a great deal, depending on factors such as whether the shop is a single owner (lower turnover), or a chain (higher turnover), or a retail or wholesale, or glamour index (video stores). It pays to know what your industry average is. After all, it's your gauge, your barometer, your measuring stick.

In Steve's company, he has the hire and fire and quit figures called in from each store, each week, along with the payrolls. As we mentioned, up to 25 percent of a manager's quarterly bonus is determined by how low he keeps the turnover. When he first implemented this bonus provision, his turnover rate dropped dramatically.

Steve is now considering bringing shift managers in addition to store managers in on this key target. As every owner knows, whatever you give a bonus for, this is what will be focused on. Thus, keeping turnover rates low is a worthy focus.

Tracking the Training Scores

The second key area in which you need to track your business activities is in your training of employees. It goes without saying that good training—inspired training, fun training—is the key to successful long-term integration of new employees, and thus to basic business success. The ideas in this book will help you discover new and effective ways of training employees. The point we want to make in this chapter is the importance of tracking the progress of this training.

When your training is tracked—that is, recorded and itemized—both trainer and trainee more quickly recognize the vital importance of such training. Top management can monitor the accumulation of various skills and expertise of the workforce. And more important, the trainee knows that he knows how to do his job because he has signed his training sheets and thus his confidence rises.

Furthermore, when there are problems or glitches in the everyday functioning of the business—shelves aren't stocked or prices are mismarked or customers are left waiting at the door—you, the manager, can look at your training records and see if such glitches might be avoided in the future by changing, rearranging, or in some way modifying the training process.

Finally, when an employee is trained right, her work is inevitably more successful, more consistent, and thus more enjoyable personally, which automatically decreases your turnover rate! Such a central factor in the equation to solve the hiring problem should not be left up to something as casual as, "By the way, did you ever get a chance to show that new guy, Willy, how to fold sweaters and jeans?"

We'll get into more details of training in later chapters, but here we want to stress the importance of tracking what training has been given, at what time, and to what degree. If you don't have such a list already, you need to make a standard chart of every task a new employee is expected to learn, in what order and at what speed.

As the employee is trained in each new task, have both the trainer and the employee initial the item, or check it off the list. Such attention to detail makes the difference between a so-so operation and a championship organization!

In Steve's business, which many of his new workers assume is a fairly simple "just make a sandwich and grin" type of business, he has over 250 separate training items, from how to fill out paperwork to how to slice a tomato, from how to run the cash register to how to service senior citizens. For example, in Steve's training manual, he has four pages devoted to cutting and preparing a tomato! He tracks the training for each employee in each one of the 250 items!

Management guru Peter Drucker wrote, "A job in which young people are not given real training . . . does not measure up to what they have a right and a duty to expect." This is true not only for young people but for *all* people! Training is a gift that your employees deserve to receive! Tracking the training ensures that both the giver and the receiver of the gift are well aware of the value exchanged.

Tracking Employee Comings and Goings

You set up forms to track your hiring process simply because you know that hiring employees is something that will be repeated regularly and you want it to run as smoothly as it possibly can. When you've done something right, you want to go back and see if you can spot what you did in the first interview. Or if you've done something wrong—hired someone you shouldn't have—you want to review the process and see if there might have been some signal at the hiring interview or in the first training stages.

Tracking your "people numbers" shouldn't end when one of your employees leaves, either. When an employee leaves, you want to know why. You want to know, if you can, where she's gone and what she's doing. A system for conducting exit interviews can be one of your most valuable tools for improving and fine-tuning your hiring and training of good employees. Exiting employees are sometimes willing to lay it on the line—to tell you what they didn't like and why they had to leave.

Those who leave within the first thirty days—which is when over 50 percent of all entry-wage turnover occurs—found something or someone, or some aspect of the business, that they simply did not or could not harmonize with their personal work desires.

Sometimes people leave simply because they have found a better job—in their own estimation of what is better, of course. You want to know, what made it better? Sometimes people leave because they didn't like the work. You want to know, what

didn't they like about the work? Sometimes people leave because the hours were wrong. What made the hours wrong? You
want to know. Sometimes they leave because the stress is too
great. Which stress? What times particularly did they feel
stressed? What if your good employees are leaving because of
one bad employee whom you had already been thinking of firing? In this current tight job market you can't afford to have such
situations. Tracking the numbers helps you avoid these pitfalls.

Since hiring hourly workers is such a problem today, become keenly interested in quantifying, wherever possible, the
circumstances that lead to turnover—an exit interview is one
fruitful place to do that. Turnover costs the average company
between $500 and $1,000 per lost employee. Doesn't it make
sense to get as much of your money back as possible?

In Steve's company, it is at the time of an employee's exit
that the manager is challenged (once again) to quantify and understand the problem. If his managers identify ten different reasons why employees quit, and reason number six is the one most
often used, then it becomes clear where creative attention must
be placed. The exit interview is probably the most underutilized
employee interview or manager's area of focus, and yet it is one
of the areas most likely to provide solutions to a company's hiring problems.

★   ★   ★   ★   ★

Numbers give you a clue as to where you are at, where you want
to go, and how you can best get there. Tracking your numbers,
not only your financial numbers but also the numbers associated
with every aspect of your business, helps clear the air and make
both your problems and your opportunities more apparent. Setting up systems to track your numbers is a necessary step in the
adventure here unfolding.

With that said, we also have to say that numbers represent
only the actions of people. It's people who are the generators of
numbers. If you don't have people, you don't have anything to
count! So what kind of people are looking for entry-wage jobs
today? Who exactly are these people who are coming to work
for you? For a fun look at the rainbow spectrum, turn to the next
chapter.

5

The Slackers, Punkers, Pranksters, Preps: How to Employ (and Enjoy!) the New Worker

You are troubled, I perceive, that your servant is run away from you; but I do not hear yet that you are either robbed or strangled or poisoned or betrayed or accused by him; so that you have escaped well in comparison with your fellows.

—Horace, 65 B.C.

As others toil for me, I must toil for others.

—Ecclesiastes 2:20

You're looking for help. But what kind of help? In Chapter 6, we're going to talk about the exciting development of the older person's return to work—or in some cases, just entering the workplace in an entry-level position (or positions that have been primarily youth jobs). This chapter, however, focuses on young people, be they goofy, gracious, gritty, gorgeous, or gruesome. We also look at young people whom you are already employing and will continue to be employing. The terms "slackers," "punkers," "pranksters," and "preps," which perhaps have a negative connotation to those outside of these groups, are the names that these groups themselves have adopted. The terms are used here only with the warm affection and good humor necessary to stay sane in this crazy environment. Slackers, punkers, pranksters, and preps—they are today's entry-wage workers.

The Ideal vs. "Real" Job Candidate

The fact that you are reading this book suggests that when you landed your first job, you were probably very excited and a little bit awed, and you secretly hoped you were up to the challenge. You probably worked hard to make a good impression. You were grateful for the opportunity, and ready to learn the rules. We suspect that you were an eager beaver, relatively speaking, wanting to do your part and do it well.

So wouldn't it be nice if you could hire a dozen or so kids who are right now just like you were back then?

Believe it or not, you can. Respectful eager-beavers are still out there. They still want to work. But with the hiring situation the way it is today, you will also find yourself hiring and working with those who represent the—shall we say—less motivated, less industrious, more cantankerous part of the spectrum. For example, in the current culture of employer-employee relations, it's now possible for a business owner to pay his Generation X employee a yearly salary of well over $2 million dollars a year and then have that employee (Utah Jazz basketball player Chris Morris) refuse to tie his shoelaces when asked! Or pay a kid (Derrick Coleman of the Philadelphia 76ers) $7.5 million a year, and then have him not show up for practice and even complain about wearing a tie on the airplane! And that's just basketball.

We've all witnessed the same type of employee problems as have those hiring the high-paid prima donnas of professional football, baseball, and even golf and tennis. An article in *Sports Illustrated* observed, "Many believe that the league's discipline problems mirror those of society, that their root is nothing less than the breakdown of the American family." The Orlando Magic's general manager Pat Williams agrees, observing that

"Young people are less tolerant of authority than they were 10, 20 years ago, and some of that can be traced back to the breakdown of the traditional family."

Of course, there's the other side of the story, which asks why you would want to harass a star athlete about tying his shoelaces or wearing a tie on the plane. Are you just trying to prove who's boss or is there a point to it? Is the reasoning old-fashioned and out of date, or is there some ethic you're trying to instill?

In a little bit we'll talk about the breakdown of the traditional family and its resulting effect on employees and potential employees. But first, let's remember that the majority of players in professional sports—as with the majority of employees in today's companies—are in fact hard workers, fairly well disciplined, and generally eager to contribute to the team.

The Ideal Worker

On September 6, 1995, Steve was fortunate enough to attend what many consider to be the greatest exhibit of the work ethic ever accomplished in sports history. Steve was at the baseball game where Cal Ripken, Jr., played his 2,131st consecutive game, breaking the fifty-five-year record held by Lou Gehrig. This was a record that many people had said would never be broken.

Cal Ripken, Jr., played fourteen years straight without missing a single game! He played 99.5 percent of every possible inning during this streak. He did it because he loved baseball. He played through pain, through slumps, through criticism from fans and the press who said he should "give it a rest." But Cal pressed on and did what no other man in over a hundred years of baseball had ever done before. We all need more "Cal Ripken" types working behind our counters!

In your business you probably have at least one or two workhorses like Cal, and then you also probably have your prima donnas, be it the soup chef, the sales rep, or the head cashier. Can you get by without the prima donnas?

No. They get that way because they are exceptionally gifted. They do attract crowds, they do break records, they do get the job done—that is, they make the business profitable. And they make the game exciting. Yes, you need them. So enjoy them. Everybody loves to have a superstar on the team. But can you get by with *only* prima donnas? Obviously not. And should they be allowed to coach the team, have their way whenever they want? Again, obviously not.

What is happening, at every level of society—from professional sports to making sub sandwiches—where we have such a wide variety of temperaments and work attitudes? If, as the media suggest, the problem is a breakdown of the traditional family, which is affecting guys who make $5 million a year, is it any wonder we're experiencing some of the same problems with people to whom we pay $5 an hour? (And reading about employee problems in professional sports, we can see that simply upping the pay is not a cure-all solution to the problem!)

So where, oh where, has the old dog gone? Let's look briefly at the nature of this supposed breakdown of the traditional family and see what it has to do with the workers you're hiring in your business, be they young or old.

New Families, New Workers

"Tonight, about 40 percent of U.S. children will go to sleep in homes in which their fathers do not live," writes David Blankenthorn, chairman of the National Fatherhood Initiative. "Fatherlessness is the engine driving our most urgent social problems, from crime to adolescent pregnancy to domestic violence." No wonder it's a challenge to teach them to stock the shelves, or to please call in when they're going to be late!

Even if 40 percent of the homes of our potential coworkers do not have fathers present—have not had fathers present—and another 5 to 10 percent have fathers living with them who just as well should be elsewhere, that still leaves 50 percent of our coworkers coming from what are considered to be the average, traditional, two-parent homes. (Even if the average, traditional home now has both parents working and the TV on for nineteen to twenty hours a day!)

So let's assume that our basic foundations are still intact, and that we need not join the nay-sayers who are complaining so much about the "aberrant" workforce they are compelled to work with. We need not buy into the doom and gloom with which we are so often presented.

The Up Side of the Single-Parent Family

And, before we go any further, it might be well to state openly and clearly that a single-parent household *need not be* the negative, dysfunctional handicap it is so often made out to be. With close to half of kids these days living in a single-parent household, we're happy to think that the traditional family of the past is now simply, and naturally, evolving into natural bipolar and tripolar support relationships: mother, brother, sister, and so on.

From our experience, we are *not* ready to write off a third to a half of our fellow youthful workers simply because they come from single-parent households. We have known young people who have come from single-parent households who have exhibited a much earlier and greater maturity, with more independence of thought, greater self-sufficiency, and greater willingness to explore new potentials (as well as a better sense of humor!), than many of their peers coming from traditional two-parent homes.

So what do we do about fatherlessness? What we can do—must do—is take advantage of this circumstance. Basically, we must agree to parent these kids—one at a time, in whatever way they need parenting.

Management's New Role

The absolute, most important thing parents can do for their children is to love them, which is the same thing as to enjoy them. And it's to love them (enjoy them), not for who they might become or for what they might bring, but for who they are already—right here, today! It's this same role that is foisted on us as managers. We must agree to take up "enjoying" these young people, right here, right now, today. That's our first and primary responsibility. This attitude is also the way to dissolve the entry-wage hiring crisis.

We're talking now about something beyond simply "accepting" these young people for who they are. We are obliged, if we really want to solve the hiring problem once and for all, to honestly *enjoy* the young people who come to work for us. Or, more precisely, we are challenged to enjoy ourselves in the midst of all of their idiosyncrasies and aberrations and needs and desires.

The Five Types of New Worker

So who is it that managers have to enjoy? We have identified five different types of new worker, each with an individual style. (Again, we are focusing on young people in this chapter. We'll do a Candid Camera of the older worker in the next chapter.) These worker types have variations, and each variation has its exceptions—no one is purely one type or another. But these are five primary groups—like food groups—that the contemporary manager will have working for her.

The five types we've identified are:

1. Straight-from-the-farm type ("I'm coming in early, 'cause I want to mop that floor . . .")
2. Straight-from-the-couch type ("Don't rush me! Besides, someone else will take care of it, sooner or later")
3. Straight-from-the-boxing-ring type ("You wanta fight about it?")
4. Straight-from-the-party type ("Hey, what's more important, work or party? Right! Let's partyyyy!")
5. Straight-from-the-ozone type ("Pardon me, which end of the pencil do you want sharpened?")

Let's look briefly at each type, and see what "potential" the manager will have to bring out from each.

Fresh off the Farm

Ahh, would that all of our new and fellow employees fall into this category. This is the Cal Ripken, Jr., type of worker, who works hard, smart, and happily, day after day, year after year. Of course, such workers do not literally come straight from the farm—except in rare instances. City and suburban people also have this work ethic, as do many recent immigrants and children of recent immigrants. But the farm is the traditional soil in which such hard, steady workers have their mythical roots.

Be they from the farm or the city or across the sea, you recognize and love the eager beaver, who is anxious to get started, hard working, respectful, easily provoked to laughter, quick to see what needs to be done, and willing to do it. This worker takes responsibility for the work on hand, whether it's assigned or not. The worker sees the wider picture—the goal and the means to reaching the goal—and is happy to be working with you, for you, toward that goal.

This worker calls when she's going to be late, but she's never late. You wish your whole company was filled with this type of worker. The only problem with this type of employee is that her future is generally so bright that it's hard to keep her content in your own little pasture. These workers move on.

The straight-off-the-farm type often knows where he wants to be in a year's time, or two years' or five years' time. So find out where these employees want to go, what they want to do, and how they want to do it. Then do everything in your power to help them along that route. Pay them well, promote them quickly, tell them and show them often that you enjoy them. Learn from them—listen and be open to their suggestions.

This whole book is about how to attract and keep just this type of worker. This worker is the ideal that you try to seek when hiring (see Chapters 8 and 9). God grant that you should have a stable full of this kind of worker.

Straight From the Couch

If there is an exact opposite to the straight-from-the-farm worker, this is it. We don't have any real proof, but our sense is that this type of worker is a fatality of the TV and Nintendo. The latest research estimates that by the age of twenty-one, a young person has watched over 10,000 hours of television. Other research shows that a person's metabolic rate while watching television is consistently slowed. Intelligence scores have been theorized to drop by 18 percent or more.

This is the kid whose parents tell him that if he doesn't get a job, they're going to cut the cable. The parents sense that the kid does need to get out and get some real-life experience—where people are actually doing something, actually moving around, actually interacting with other people. The parents' survival instinct for their child is what pushes them to push the kid to come calling on your doorstep.

Too much television explains the glassy eyes, the slow walk, the thick comprehension, the jaw hanging open. We've all had employees like this, and we've all been waited on—served—by employees like this. Many of these straight-from-the-couch kids are afflicted with what Zig Zigler, the renowned motivational speaker (and author of *See You at the Top* and other bestsellers), calls "stinkin' thinkin'." There's nothing that will rob your energy quicker, more efficiently than "stinkin' thinking," which is basically thinking those thoughts, telling yourself those stories that you don't really enjoy. TV is full of them. You simply can't learn life's most valuable lessons by watching TV!

But the good news is that some of these kids actually do wake up! You never know which one it's going to be, but occasionally one of them, after working for a while, under the influence of precise and deliberate training, after being around real-live humans doing real active work, one or two or three of them actually come out of the daze! And then you have a good worker on your payroll, right up there with the straight-from-the-farm type.

The secret for waking up these kids is, first, to stick with your own joy. Enjoy them, even in their slow motion. Enjoy them, even in all their sluggishness. You can do that only by first enjoying yourself—insisting that the only thoughts which you yourself will entertain are those thoughts that you enjoy.

Many of these kids are looking for a sense of self-worth. They pick this up when their coworkers start enjoying them as they already are, and as others see their potential. It's tempting when dealing with this straight-from-the-couch type to become irritated, frustrated, and impatient. Remember, the most important thing for you and for everybody around you is for you to enjoy your own happiness. This is, after all, the Law of Happiness.

The manager who can make these "couchers" wake up is a manager who is performing a multilevel, multidimensional service. Not only are these managers useful to the business, they are useful to the coucher himself. And they are useful to society as a whole. This manager's joy is important. The joy is a healing influence. Don't let the couchers dim it!

Straight From the Boxing Ring

Many young people have learned to identify themselves with the intensity of combat—conflict—they provoke. The more aggressive they are, the more alive they feel. For many of these "fighters," it's not the winning or losing that energizes them, but rather simply being in the fight. Curiously, these fighters will as easily assume the role of victim as of victor. In fact, more often than not, they come on as victims, since the job is so readily available.

It's hard for a manager to continue enjoying herself while the victim is presenting her case about her most recent problem. And yet, this is exactly what needs to be done. The manager needs to recognize that the fight that the employee has recently encountered, in spite of all appearances, is only inside the fighter's head! Getting involved in fights and squabbles is always a result of a person's thinking what she does not enjoy thinking—of purposely *not* enjoying the words and actions of others.

So what do you do as a manager when you encounter this type of employee? On the one hand, you continue to practice your own joy. You refrain from joining in the fight, either for or against. You refuse to entertain thoughts that you don't enjoy. And often, when you can spot them ahead of time, it means *not* hiring this type of fighter-victim in the first place. This is the easiest way to keep the peace.

On the other hand, when you find you have one or more such people already on your staff, you train them out of it! You explain to the victim exactly what you are doing! You not only demonstrate, you also teach—formally or informally—the four principles of joy, the Be Happy Game.

Specifically, this means you tell the person flat out: Enjoying yourself is the most important thing for you and for everybody else. You help the person to see what thoughts, exactly, he is thinking that he is not enjoying, and rather than simply giving him thoughts or stories that he might enjoy better, you train him to create, to discover thoughts on his own that he enjoys more. You help him to begin managing his own thoughts, just as you manage yours.

Many of the fighter-victims you will encounter in the workplace are in fact "primed" for the introduction of a tool like this to make their lives so much easier. Being a victim is a hard, lonely, emotionally and physically draining habit. Many victims are easily taught the four basic principles for inner management of their lives. And they are grateful for the opportunity to find their way out of that maze of stress.

Straight From the Party

Contrary to the teachings of most of our culture, we don't need to do anything to become happy, according to Christian Almayrac, originator of the Be Happy Game. "We already are naturally happy. Happiness is our original state of being. We can either choose to enjoy that state, or we choose to forget it."

"Party hardy" types are often locked into the belief that they must be doing something—generally involved with stimulating their senses—in order to "feel happy." They believe in drugs, sex, and rock and roll as a way to salvation. They push the hardest for rock music at work, and their conversations are focused on either last night's party, next weekend's concert, or the newest fad or craze in pop culture. If they aren't actually stimulating their senses, then talking about it is the next best thing. Such "seasons" are apparently necessary for many young people in order for them to experience first hand the truth that stimulating the senses does not equate to automatic happiness!

As we've mentioned, you are, to a degree, a parental figure for your employees. It's work thrust upon you by the times. At some point, however, you simply cannot assume this final responsibility, from either a legal, social, or business perspective. When an employee is too much, too often in the party mode, you have no choice but to let the person go (see Chapter 13). For some of these young people, such experiences are a necessary part of their learning process.

Nevertheless, you will be employing at least a few party types who hold the assumption—which to a certain extent is true—that what they do in their own time is their own business. So the most generous, most helpful thing you as a manager can do is to share the life secret that "thinking what you are happiest thinking" is in the end the only way people ever truly enjoy themselves. You can be a source of strength for these young people. Don't ever be a stick-in-the-mud, no-never, not-me type. Rather, be a whole, happy, complete human being who truly does know a bit of life's wisdom. Just like a parent!

But, in the meantime, what do you do with the party types while they're at work? They're often very animated, quite intelligent, very industrious. Obviously, the best thing to do is to enjoy them. Not necessarily to support them in their partying, but to enjoy them for who they are, what they are doing.

And make your training fun. Make work fun. Make your relationships with them light and easy and breezy, without being "undisciplined." Stay with them, in their ups and downs. Enjoy them. Be there with them (and put smoke detectors in the bathroom).

Straight From the Ozone

For better or worse, we have aliens on earth. Or if not aliens, then the alienated. These are people who are not satisfied with the seemingly agreed-upon reality, the agreed-upon social norms. Some of them are so alien—so alienated—that the prospect of actually working for an employer is close to nil.

These people are not in the same time-space continuum as you are. They don't usually apply for jobs. Or when they do apply, they come in covered with white face cream, black lipstick, purple hair, a black leather jacket with the sleeves cut off, and no eyebrows. You have a clue, from the get-go, that this one might not work out.

Others are still sufficiently tied in to the three-dimensional world that they recognize the need to earn some money, and they appear ordinary enough in enough consecutive moments that it seems OK to hire them. It's only then you realize you've hired an alien. (Actually, we love 'em. They often make the day seem lollapoolooza light, just when you need it.)

There's a goofy, low-budget movie available on videotape called *Clerks* (View Askew Productions). We especially recommend it to business owners and store managers for its view of what the ozone worker is doing when you're not there. *Clerks* is a Generation X movie—or more precisely, a slackers flick. (Slackers are a subgroup within Generation X.) The film portrays a day at the Quick Stop Grocery Store, which happens to have a movie rental store next door. The clerks are two young men who manage the businesses while managing their lives, not in that order! It's raunchy and wacky and raucous, and captures—if in exaggeration—the alienation of young kids whom you must learn to work with, and depend on—and enjoy—if you are to employ the new type of worker!

In the film, a sign on the shop counter reads: PLEASE LEAVE MONEY ON THE COUNTER. TAKE CHANGE WHEN APPLICABLE. BE HONEST. The dialogue is as follows:

"Hey Charlie, you have a customer."

"Yea, what do you want?"

After "helping" the customer, the clerk comments, "This job would be great if it weren't for the [bleeping] customers."

"You ever notice how all the prices end in '9 . . . ?"

"I'm stuck here 'till closing."

"If we're so advanced, what are we doing working in a place like this?"

There's a certain malaise, a nihilism among young people today that is showing up in our young workforce. If you haven't read the book *Slacker*, it is worth searching it out. Even more than Generation X, it reveals a certain approach to life that is more and more common in the young people coming to work for us.

A lot of the workers from the ozone are some of the most intelligent of this generation. They have not been taught to see real meaning, real future, real progress in the society around them, and thus they are not willing to put their lives on line for something that they do not feel has any meaning. And who can blame them?

As a manager, the work—the challenge—is for you to enjoy this type of person, too. Enjoy the malaise. Enjoy the disenchantment. Enjoy the shallow appeal. Enjoy with gusto, with animation, with sound-as-a-rock happiness. These people, too, can be awakened. Surprisingly, when you start training these ozone kids, they dig it. They often like the hard and solid reality of daily work. Many of them have never been given such work before, and they are pleasantly surprised to find themselves performing a service that others need. They find themselves needed, often for the first time in their lives. And this they can appreciate. This is the human family. You make them part of your team, and the world is a better place for it.

★　★　★　★　★

These five different types of young worker can be found in almost every job. Of course, there is rarely a pure ozone or a pure off-the-farm. You'll find varying degrees of each type in all of your workers.

You've probably noticed, however, that the key to unlocking potential is the joy that you, as their manager, maintain. Joy is the common ground as well as the common goal. As the philosopher William James wrote, "How to gain, how to keep, how to recover Happiness is in fact, for most people at all times the secret motive for all they do and all they are willing to endure."

In the end, you don't need to remember the five types of employees, if you only remember your own joy. This is the key to managing all these types effectively. Let's take a look, now, at the older worker who is just entering, or is reentering, the workforce and will be working with these five types of employees.

6

Get a Job, Grandma!

*We grow neither better nor worse as we get old, but
more like ourselves.*

—Mary Lamberton Becker

Teenagers love to hang out at the mall, right? Right. It's a universal phenomenon.

So when Steve opened his Subway Sandwich Store in the major shopping mall of our city—the one where all the teens of our town hung out—he assumed he'd have no problem filling the job openings. After all, a part-time job would give the teens a legitimate excuse for going to the mall, being at the mall, seeing their friends, give them a working part in the "mall action." And money to boot!

Many of you already know what we're going to say: It didn't work out that way. Steve had a harder time filling those slots than any other store in the city. Why? Who knows. Maybe it was the stigma of actually working in front of friends— wearing the uniform in front of friends, being a "servant" to friends. So the mall store was where he started concentrating on hiring older workers. And now he is glad he did.

There's still a certain stigma regarding the older worker in entry-level and/or lower-wage jobs. As the next century dawns, however, that stigma will rapidly disappear. Ten years ago it was rare to find anybody over thirty working in the entry-level positions of the quick-service or mass-marketing industries, be they restaurants, convenience stores, or retail outlets. It was generally assumed that people in such positions had probably been left there—or served in some similar position with another company for many years—simply because they did not have the necessary social or intellectual skills to advance with their peers.

That's clearly not the case anymore. With the decrease in available young people, and the increase in available entry-level job openings, it's only natural that employers are encouraging—coaxing, begging, pleading—older people to fill the slots. For the purpose of this book, we define the older worker as anyone from the mid-thirties on up. Obviously, mid-thirties is *not* old—not even middle age—except in comparison to the average age of entry-level workers.

In the early 1990s, the McDonald's Corporation made a conscious decision to go after the older worker, and has had amazing success. McDonald's has even consciously focused on putting older employees into their television commercials. (Oh, you've noticed?) It's a step in helping break down stereotypes.

Nevertheless, we are still early enough into this phenomenon of older workers in entry-wage positions that it is still the manager's job to help older workers enjoy the business at hand, and help them overcome the lingering social stigma still attached to the entry-level or lower-wage position. Prejudices are slow to dissipate, and yet they are indeed dissipating. We are finding more and more older workers in our stores and restaurants, and this development must be recognized as good and healthy for business, for the economy, and for society as a whole.

So as you try to lure the older worker out of the closet and into your workplace, it's helpful to recognize the three places from which they most often come.

Mothers Entering or Reentering the Workplace

This is by far the largest pool from which you will draw older workers. The age group of these mothers varies greatly, from mid-thirties to late-fifties. Most of these reentering mothers have been devoting years to raising children and keeping a home, and now for one reason or another they are ready to work in the business sector. These mothers have children anywhere from ages six to sixteen or older.

Also, with the divorce rate a high as it is, it's fair to admit that a significant percentage of these women are entering the workplace out of necessity. Although many of these women will often become the best workhorses you have, it is well to be aware that single mothers have a 33 percent higher absence rate than nonsingle mothers. Be forewarned; that way, you won't get as uptight when it happens. (Note: Employment laws stipulate that you *cannot* ask whether an applicant has children at home or whether she is married. It is construed as a form of job discrimination.)

And here's a second warning: When a person is going through marital separation, the experience unleashes forces not always easily tamed by the routines of the workplace. You may discover that your best worker has decided, overnight, that she's going to move back to Des Moines and start over—this afternoon! But this is no different from the high school guy who decides he's going out for football "this afternoon!" Or the store manager who goes to Phoenix, chasing after his ex-girlfriend "this afternoon." So the returning mom is just as viable, although perhaps just as volatile, as any other worker you may hire.

Retired Workers Returning to the Workforce

Although this group of people is often the first "pool" that people think about when imagining the older worker, it is, in fact, the smallest source of employees. When they do go back to work, most retired people have particular, specialized interests and hobbies that they want to pursue and/or old friends in the industry who present them with part-time employment opportunities. Nevertheless, with changes in Social Security and Medicare allowing for more income, more retirees are reentering the workplace to supplement their income and reinvolve themselves with the activity of business.

The first reason retired people return to work is often the hidden reason: Even ten hours a week at $5 an hour makes life a lot easier. But contrary to popular notion, recent studies have shown that only 12 percent of the elderly claim that money troubles are significant worries for them.

The second reason retirees accept entry-level jobs—wanting to involve themselves again in the workaday world—is the motivation behind most reentering workers. They want to be useful again. They want to be "hooked in." They want the companionship.

As with returning mothers, retirees can prove to be steady, reliable workers offering many years of productive service. However, proposed laws mandating employer-sponsored health insurance for even part-time workers may throw a monkey wrench into this arena. If mandated insurance premiums continue to be based on age, then employers will quietly, but inevitably, *not* hire older workers. This would result in "mandated" age discrimination unless insurance companies are likewise required to insure anyone, at the same premium, regardless of age or physical condition.

There is a relatively small pool of retired workers coming back into the entry-level work environment, but this pool is rich with potential. In a moment we'll discuss ways to tap into it.

People Who Are Repositioning, Relocating, Redirecting

One of the best workers we ever had was a man who had been an alcoholic for over thirty years. When he came to us he had been sober for over four years. And although he wasn't the quickest, and he wasn't the most intelligent worker, he was the most dedicated, the most persistent, and the most respectful.

People do fall on hard times. And we, as business owners and managers, are sometimes in a position to give them a hand up. People going through divorce, or those who have had a history of trouble—prison, physical disabilities, mental problems, and so on—may become very valuable resources. This arena obviously requires case-by-case decisions. Alert, sensitive, open-minded, realistic managers are needed to make these types of decisions.

As this book is being written, proposals are before Congress that would mandate that welfare recipients accept entry-level work or lose their eligibility for subsidies. As entry-level employers, we are being considered part of the solution to the high costs of the "welfare state." It will be interesting to see how this unfolds, and if "forced labor" is indeed forced upon the employer as well. The solution, then, will come in attitudinal training.

Traps to Avoid Regarding Older Workers

Although hiring Grandma or Grandpa would seem to be the fastest and easiest ticket to success in your business, there are a handful of problems that can result if your management policies aren't even-handed. Consider these five easy pitfalls that may trap the unwary manager.

1. *Promoting Too Fast*

There's a natural tendency to want to promote new older workers right away. It's important to promote them as quickly as they are ready—you don't want to bore them or make them feel trapped. But make sure they are working at the level they are comfortable at, which they enjoy.

2. *Overprotection From Rowdy Youth*

Younger managers especially have a tendency to want to protect their older employees from the craziness of young people. The young manager often gives the older worker responsibilities that isolate her from the normal routines of the day. Generally, this comes from underestimating the life experience of the older worker and overestimating the callousness of the corps.

3. *No Protection From the Rowdy Youth*

The other extreme occurs when managers pretend that Grandma is just like the kids. Or she should be. And if she doesn't like listening to Dead Milkmen on the radio, or if she doesn't enjoy the food fights after work, well, she just better learn!

4. *Lowering Standards for Older Workers*

Believe it or not, Grandma or Grandpa can be lazy! And they can talk too much or work at too slow a pace or call in sick when they really want to just stay home and drink tea. They're just like a human being! But it's sometimes hard to discipline your mom, or your dad—which is what some younger managers feel they are doing when they discipline their older workers. So they don't do it. They just let it slide.

But the other workers will notice and resent it. And soon their own work habits will start to slide in order to match the standards of the older worker. This happens much more quickly with the poor work habits of an older worker than poor habits of a younger worker.

5. *Working Them Too Hard*

This is the other side of the lower-standards trap. Sometimes young managers find an older worker who is more than willing to do anything he is asked, and thus the young manager inveigles the older worker to do all the work that the others won't. And/or the older worker will do work that needs to be done before he is asked, and the manager naturally appreciates it. And after a while comes to expect it. In such a case, the standards for the older worker are not lower, but higher than for the rest of the crew.

Why It's Smart to Employ Older Workers

Now let's take a look at the joys—the benefits—of hiring the older worker. These are numerous and common—and so obvious they need little explanation:

10 Reasons to Employ the Older Worker

1. They are generally more dependable about keeping hours.
2. They are often more conscientious on the job.
3. They are consistently less likely to job-hop.
4. When they do leave, they are more likely to give sufficient notice.
5. Their presence generally provides a healthy balance to younger workers, and thus balances the working environment.
6. The presence of older workers gives a feel of balance to customers. And older workers are often oriented more to customer service and communication.
7. The accumulated life skills of older workers will often rub off on younger workers.
8. Their previous job and life experiences often bring new insights and valuable suggestions to managers, which help solve current business problems.
9. They've often learned, and are able to share, what is most important in life—humor, compassion, simple joys—thus they are most often a pleasure to work with.
10. The older worker typically has more respect, more understanding, and more patience with your business than does the younger person.

In touting the virtues of the older worker, we don't want to get into the trap of reverse discrimination. We could have just as easily come up with ten reasons to employ the younger worker, but that would have seemed prejudicial.

How Do You Attract Older Workers?

Finding older workers for your business is not always a matter of running some classified ads and waiting for the applicant to show up. This pool of potential employees is often reached via other means.

1. *Ask for them in your ads.* Ask for this employee outright in your ads and in your recruiting literature. A simple tag line, "Older workers encouraged to apply," can be very effective. As the scriptures promise, "Ask, and you shall receive."

2. *Post job openings at senior centers.* This is obvious, but in fact it is a seldom used approach that can generate many applications.

3. *Send announcements to medical professionals and health centers.* Medical doctors and other health practitioners are very much aware of the senior population—both their potentials and their limitations—and can be excellent referral sources for appropriate employees.

4. *Post job openings in "mature living" complexes.* We're not talking about nursing homes or retirement homes here, but rather about those complexes—apartment complexes, mobile home parks, condominiums—that are tailored to the older resident.

5. *Send announcements to local churches.* Contact local clergy members, with a cover letter suggesting that you are willing to hire older workers and those who are just now reentering the workforce. The clergy are often a good source for referrals for the "mother returning to work" category. As with the medical doctors, they generally won't make a referral of someone who is too troubled to hold a job.

6. *Show off your older workers.* If you hire older workers but keep them in the background, keep them out of sight, then your more mature customers won't think of your place as an option for potential employment. Hire older workers and be proud of it! Make sure your customers see them.

7. *Ask your older workers for referrals.* This is the same as asking your younger workers for referrals. Most older people are part of a well-established network of family and friends, and are eager to help others in their network who are in need of work.

8. *Stress schedule flexibility and stability.* In your job announcements, make sure people realize that the position has flexible hours with stability. Although, as you'll discover, older workers and mothers returning to the workforce are some of the

most regular, dependable workers you will have, they also have a high need for flexibility in their schedules. Or sometimes, and even more important, they want stability, where you are not changing their hours. You'll discover that with the older worker, flexibility is generally not a "spur of the moment" thing the way it often is with younger workers. Rather, they will let you know that two weeks from Tuesday they need to have the morning off between 10 and 12.

Stability of schedule—regular hours week after week—is sometimes even more important, and can often be used to lure the older worker. For example, "Now Hiring—Seniors Welcome. 10:30–1:30, Tuesdays, Wednesdays, Thursdays."

9. *Keep a clean environment.* A clean environment is an important key for both young and older workers. Obviously, the way we attract and keep older workers is not that much different—though it can be a little different—from the way we keep younger workers. We're not suggesting that the older worker necessarily likes a clean environment more than a younger worker. But on the other hand, the difference between Grandma's bedroom and your average teenager's bedroom. . . .

10. *Enjoy your work, enjoy your workers.* As mentioned already, your being happy is the key to attracting and keeping any good worker, but it bears repeating here. Joy is what keeps us young. Joy is what makes us attractive. Joy is what is profitable. Joy is what is interesting.

Older workers are happy to come to work for younger managers, but if the manager is always uptight, always worried, always nervous about the way things are working, then the older worker feels drained of energy. (As does everybody!) The older worker won't put up with it as long. She recognizes the life force being drained, although she may not clearly understand that it's a lack of joy that's doing it.

A Few Warning Signs

It's only fair to admit that you must look out for a few warning signs when hiring an older worker. They are generally the same signs that you'll want to guard against in the younger worker, but they nevertheless should be repeated here.

1. *Stinkin' thinkin'.* This is negative, unhappy, *woe is me* type of thinking. Such thinking can be present at any age. When it's prevalent in an older worker, it's a lot more difficult to dissolve.

2. *Poor me—I really need this job.* This is just a particular type of stinkin' thinkin', but it's worth separating out because it's such a clear sign of difficult times ahead. That's because a poor-me script doesn't change just because the person has found a job. Something else will be the cause of "poor me." And most likely it will be the job itself!

3. *I'm looking for a place to coast.* . . . Sometimes the older worker has been "broken," is no longer looking to help out, is no longer interested in building anything, is no longer wanting to advance himself. That's OK, but not while on your payroll!

4. *I'm taking only thirty-five pills a day and seeing the doctor only twice a week.* . . . You need to be alert to people whose main interest, as revealed in their conversation, is bodily illness—past, present, and future. Until we learn to use joy more efficiently, in all that we do, our bodies will still keep wearing out. (Joy retards aging!) But it's not so much the actual health condition that is worrisome as it is the attitude about health that is important.

★   ★   ★   ★   ★

So, isn't this a fairly balanced picture of the older worker? You don't need to view the older worker as the final answer to all of your problems. Nor should you decide to never again hire the old codgers. The point is that older workers are valuable, resourceful human beings. You would be missing a great deal if you didn't hire them regularly, repeatedly. After all, you yourself are a day older today than you were yesterday! So enjoy!

With that said, let's move on to the next chapter, where you'll learn how to inspire more people—more potential employees of all ages—to walk through your doors, looking for work.

7

Help for Your Help Wanteds

It's the worm that lures the fish, not the fisherman and his tackle.

—Angler's maxim

You have undoubtedly already been using the help wanted ads to generate new applicants. Such advertising is basic business communication. But if your experience with the classifieds is anything like the rest of the country, you've been frustrated with the results of these ads in the past couple of years. On the whole, your ads are probably generating fewer responses, from less qualified people, even when the ads are run for longer periods of time. Welcome to the hiring crunch.

According to recent surveys by the U.S. Labor Department and the National Ad Council, 60 to 90 percent of all your new help is still going to come to you as a result of your help wanted advertisements. This remains the primary marketplace where buyers and sellers of entry-wage labor most often come together.

But as you've undoubtedly noticed, these ads, especially those run in large city newspapers, are becoming more and more expensive while generating fewer responses. Once last year, we placed $500 worth of advertisements in a large daily paper and received only five responses. That's $100 per response! It simply doesn't pay.

So we did a study of what worked and what didn't work. Our intent was to get more bang for our buck, see if we could generate at least twice the response for half the cost. We did. And here's how we did it.

The Hardest Job in the World

You need to take a good, hard look at some classified ads you've run recently. This time, look at them from the vantage point of your potential applicant.

Remember, browsing through the help wanteds is a person's first step in finding a job. Such browsing (which for some people may go on for weeks or months!) is much easier than actually going out and knocking on doors, submitting applications. If someone should happen to come knocking on your door, without the impetus of an ad, quick—sit down with her! Listen to her, ask what she's looking for, then woo her into your business. A "door knocking" applicant is often a very motivated, very "timely" employee! (More about this in Chapter 9.) Most potential employees, however, won't come knocking on your door without an invitation. That's because the hardest job in the world is looking for a job.

Help wanted ads take some of the strain off seeking employment. It's a lot easier for people looking for a job to simply read the help wanted columns in the safety of their home. In reading the ads, they don't have to talk to strangers, at least not yet; those employers won't say yay or nay, at least not yet; and so the applicants won't be rejected, at least not yet. They can just browse for a new identity!

That browsing in itself is tough work. If you keep that in mind when you make up your ads, your responses will improve. As paradoxical as it may sound, the difficulty of looking for new work is one of the reasons managers don't get as many responses as they think they might. It's tough on these kids—and older workers, too—to browse through the help wanteds while simultaneously scanning, judging, and rejudging their own talents, potentials, and previous performances. Just reading the help wanteds is, like the cartoonists imply, both mentally and emotionally draining.

So your goal with your help wanted ad is to make it as easy as you can for these people to get up out of their chairs and actually contact you, to get them to respond to your ad before responding to any of the other dozens of ads they might also be considering.

The Basics of a Good Ad

What makes them choose your ad over the others they see? There are a number of factors, but here are some basics to include in your help wanted ads that should help you generate more responses. Each of your classified ads should include the following items.

An Attention Grabber

We're sorry to say, but the name of your establishment is generally *not* a grabber! (WILLIE'S VIDEO RENTALS IS NOW HIRING . . .) You know what kind of employee you want, so come up with half a dozen ideas of what would grab the attention of *that employee!* With the help wanteds the way they are, you need an attention grabber in the first five lines to make your ad stand out from all the others on the page.

For example, Kean Brothers, a discount gasoline and convenience chain in Chicago, was looking for managers and assistant managers. The company knew exactly what type of people they were looking for and showed it with the bold, simple, attention-grabbing headline, RUN YOUR OWN SHOW! The first thing the applicant is asked to think about in this ad is himself—running his own show, being his own boss. That makes it easy to attract the people who want to do exactly that.

The Straight Talk

Don't be so clever that you never tell people that you are looking for a night manager, or somebody who can lift fifty pounds, or work under water, or whatever. This "straight talk" is what most help wanteds contain, but you'd be surprised how often the essentials are left out. Counter Sales for Plumbing Wholesaler. That's the straight stuff!

On the other hand, if you put in too much meat, you may screen out too many people. You're better off getting too many responses than not enough. Having too many specifics is a rare problem, but if you haven't been pulling the numbers you'd like, you may need to simplify your ad. Some people who may actually fit well into your organization are being scared away by the number of requirements the ad implies. Let them see you face-to-face. You can also see them face-to-face—and decide whether you are suited for each other.

A Surprising, Gentle, or Human Twist

By a gentle or human twist we mean something humane, something "me to you." Something interesting! If you want to attract interesting and pleasantly surprising applicants, then your ads have to be interesting and pleasantly surprising. Fair is fair!

In an ad in *The Washington Post*, Bob's Stores started with a drawing of a crabby man, yelling, with the headline To Avoid a Boss Like This . . . Get A Job at Bob's. Nobody likes a crabby boss. This ad promised pleasant, humane working conditions.

Some Common Ground

Present the human side of your business, with your focus on the applicant rather than on you, the employer. Mention the flexibility of hours, or that seniors are encouraged, or your pleasant working conditions, great customers, free lunches, whatever. What would a "regular Joe" like about working at your place?

In the *Arizona Republic*, a wallpaper company asked, Are Your Walls Closing In On You? Get out of your house and come to us. They found a clever common ground between their company work and their potential applicant. Remember, focus on the applicant!

A Call for Action

An action call generally means a time constraint, or telling potential applicants which days, which hours, to contact you. Take it another step and give them a name, Ask for Willie . . . Or tell them to bring in a resume or call for more information. Asking for action is like moving toward the close of this hiring transaction.

Let us share an ad that simultaneously breaks most of the

traditional rules and subtly respects the rules and, in the end, keeps the most important rule of all: Generate a great response!

ALLIGATORS!

> We are interested in hiring 3 semi-obnoxious, pushy Acct. Executives for a very boring repetitive job of selling. Our rather dismal office is located in L——. You would be forced to work in the office. Our current staff, which is the laziest group of individuals you will ever see, drag themselves to work 5 days a week to decide whether to complain about the weather, the coffee, the thermostat or the manager. When that's all over, they sometimes manage to organize themselves, work their calls and sell a whole lot of our services. Which is surprising, because our prices are too high and the economy stinks. Applicants should have skin like an Alligator, and a desire to suffer their way to make at least a thousand a week. Call collect. 303–555–5555. Ask for Mr. Jones.

Some people think this ad is obnoxious. Others love it. Tom Graham, the sales manager who wrote it, first used it when he was working in Oklahoma for a company selling memberships in camping resorts. (How many responses can *you* generate for a job selling camping memberships?) Over the last ten years he's changed industries numerous times, but he takes the ad with him to new locales selling different products, and the ad keeps working.

"It gets the phone ringing," he says. "Then it's up to whoever answers the phone to take the enquiries and turn them into honest applicants."

The traditional notion is that humor is very difficult to pull off in a classified ad, and that it should therefore not be tried. That's especially true if you have to go through a publications committee to get the advertisement approved. Committees are notorious for having no sense of humor! The Alligator ad contains most of the first five basics: a grabber, some meat, surprise twists, a human dimension, and a call for action. The boss was able to poke fun at himself. He didn't pretend that his business was the most important thing since oxygen. It was well designed, with a first grabber and an ending grabber (hinting at

$1,000 a week). It was conversational in tone. All of these things are excellent qualities in an ad.

Clearly, this would *not* be the ad to use if you were selling burial services, mainframe computers, or Boeing 767s. But we include it here to help you stretch your notion of what you might do in your adverts.

Your Personal or Company Vision

You make reference to your company's vision or purpose so as to attract the right applicant and screen out the others. Part of attracting the right applicant is saying something clear, honest, and upbeat about the culture of your business: who you are, what you believe, where you're heading.

The classified ad is in some ways your own resume. Whether you share your vision at the beginning or at the end of the ad depends on your style. Test it both ways and see which one pulls more responses.

SUCCESS NEVER GOES OUT OF STYLE begins an ad for store managers for the Denver-based company Bed Bath and Beyond. In the next paragraph, they tell how the company's net sales have soared 44 percent, capping five consecutive years of double-digit growth, and they're celebrating an unprecedented 10.5 percent increase in same-store sales for December! Clearly, this company is looking for managers who enjoy working with numbers and with setting numerical goals, people who already understand basic retail jargon. The ad will attract those who can identify with the vision and screen out those who don't.

STAY IN RETAIL AND HAVE A LIFE suggests an ad in the *Dallas Morning News* for Colbert Stores, a premier retailer of ladies apparel, known throughout Dallas and the State of Texas. The ad continues with:

> COLBERT'S is known for great service and a fine selection
> of merchandise. Naturally we want great associates. If you
> consider yourself the best, you'll find a home at COLBERT'S.

If you doubt your abilities, you're not going to respond to this ad. If you consider yourself fairly classy and want to upgrade to a fancier store, you're likely to respond.

A quick word of caution, however. You don't want to spec-
ify age, sex, marital status, or any other potentially discrimina-
tory qualifications. We are allowed to be discriminating, but not
to discriminate against a person's natural characteristics.

An Easy Way to Apply

Your ad should make it easy for the applicant to apply. No
phone calls please is one way to screen out a lot of people, and is
generally not the best approach to getting your positions filled.
However, when you do allow phone contacts for the position,
then you are also going to have to assign someone to take those
calls. And that person should be one of your best communica-
tors or salespersons. Don't make it one more burden for an already overworked employee.

Some companies have started sending applications to people who call, along with brochures about the company (resumes!) and the various attractions of working for them. Others
have offered to give a "first interview" over the phone. The company spokesperson asks some questions and fills out the initial
forms, in order to get a relationship going. (You'll read more
about this in Chapter 9.)

If accepting phone calls from applicants is unworkable for
you, you can still make it easy for potential employees to contact
you. Give them specific hours, specific days, and specific names
to ask for so there's no question as to when and how to take the
first step. For example, Safeway Grocery Stores provides a job
hotline for callers, and also indicates that applications can be
picked up any time at any Safeway store. Glamour Shots, a national high-fashion photography chain, provides a toll-free
number to call to arrange for an interview. Home Depot likes to
hold job fairs over a several-day time period when they open a
new store to give potential applicants a wide window of opportunity. What could be easier than going to the fair?

The point is to recognize that looking for work *is* hard work,
and that your job is to make that work easier, in whatever way
you can.

Realistic Promises

A large reason for the high turnover rate in today's job market
is that the expectations of new employees are often not met.

Don't get so carried away with your advertisement that you oversell the organization. If you do, the applicant will soon realize she has been sold a bill of goods. This overpromising is not only unfair to the employee, it is also costly to you in terms of turnover costs.

Ideally, what you want to happen is that, as the worker gets to know your business better during the first two weeks, she is more and more impressed with all the benefits, the goodwill, the atmosphere. In sales there is a well-known phenomenon called *buyer's remorse*. No matter how fancy or how functional a product, the buyer, after having shopped around and finally bought, will very often feel a certain let-down in the days immediately following because of all the other products or services that he didn't buy, which he had considered in his buying decision.

The same thing often happens when a new employee has "bought" into the job you offered. This buyer's remorse is why 50 percent of turnover occurs in the first thirty days! The buyer's remorse is intensified if there has been overpromise and underdelivery. This is why many new employees get the urge to move on, before (to them) it's too late!

Telephone sales companies seem especially prone to overpromising, suggesting $15 to $50 AN HOUR DOING EASY TELEPHONE SURVEYS! A closet-organizer store advertised for CREATIVE, ENERGETIC, MAYBE EVEN A LITTLE COMPULSIVE people, saying that in their store, THE PACE IS QUICK, ENERGY IS HIGH, DETAIL IS EVERYTHING, THE SCHEDULE IS ANYTHING BUT 9 TO 5. It's actually a nice ad, but what happens when the new employee is standing in an empty store on a snowy Tuesday afternoon, wondering where the excitement is?

You have to put your best foot forward. But don't get carried away. Stick with your joy—it'll give you a clear signal as to what is enough, and what is too much!

Tracking Your Responses

It is essential that your ads be tracked and tested! Sunday paper help wanteds do generally, but not always, generate more responses than ads run on Thursdays or Fridays. And longer ads do generally, but not always, pull more responses than shorter ads. Publishing your starting hourly wage does generally, but not always, attract more applicants than not publishing these wages. You need to test to find the right balance between too many and not enough specifics in your ads.

The goal is to generate a minimum of three to four times as many applicants as you have openings. The only way you can know if you are reaching that goal is to track the ads. Writing creative ads is both a science and an art, but tracking and testing those ads is pure science. You need to have numbers: How many responses? How soon do they start coming in? Which ads generate how many new employees? Which days? How long since you last ran that same ad? What's the difference between running the same ad twice and running different ads at different times?

Finding the answers to these questions—keeping records in a scientific manner—helps you refine your art. We recommend keeping an ordinary spiral notebook with the details—names, dates, places—of each component in the help wanted process. Devote one page simply to recording which ads you placed on which dates, and how long the ads were run. Then devote separate pages to recording the number of telephone responses or walk-in responses. A third page can be devoted to tracking the number of first interviews, the questions asked, and the time it took for each interview. Then you record how many hires you generated from each ad.

You may have other details you want to follow—for example, the number of males compared to females who responded, oldsters versus youngsters, college-educated versus high school dropouts. Only by keeping such records can you gain a useful, accurate picture of the true results of your help wanted advertising. Once you have six months' worth of advertising documented in your notebook, you will find yourself studying it, amazed to find patterns emerging, insights and warning flags that you otherwise might never have suspected.

An example of one way to improve your responses, which we discovered through tracking, is to place your ads in different sections of the newspaper. For example, we place our ads in the sports section, the home section, or the entertainment section.

How do we know that our applicants responded to those ads? We *asked* them where they saw it!

We are amazed that some companies, which extensively track their coupons and special incentives, don't track the success of their help wanted ads. And yet this is the most expensive "product" they have!

We know that once you begin keeping your numbers—and, more important, become interested and excited about your numbers crunching—you'll find that you start making small, seemingly insignificant adjustments. Before long you will start pulling in a larger number of applicants.

★ ★ ★ ★ ★

If you follow the guidelines in this chapter, you'll be amazed at the positive turnabout in your hiring situation. In the next chapter, we'll look at what other things you might do—besides the help wanteds—to increase the number of applicants for openings at your business.

8

Guerrilla Hiring Tricks

If your help wanteds aren't cost-efficient, or if the competition for workers in the classifieds is just too great for your business, you have to find other ways to bring in job applicants. Or even if your help wanteds have started to work (using the tips in Chapter 7), it's only prudent to continue to broaden your base and build new "supply lines" to ensure plenty of workers.

Some managers complain that "it's a jungle out there" trying to find new help. If you *are* in a jungle, you need to employ, or at least be aware of, not only some guerrilla tactics—hit and run hiring for the least expense—but also some monkey, baboon, jaguar, and boa constrictor tactics—all of which you may not want to employ but you may find others employing against you!

There's never any reason to stop creating opportunities for potential employees to contact you, unless you are already just full to overflowing with applicants. So this chapter suggests different ways to hire outside of the help wanted columns. These ideas are presented here to prime the pump, to get your own creative juices flowing. The best ideas are the ones you get excited about and have the most fun with.

Guerrilla Tactics for Finding New Hires

Even though we offer some crazy ideas, most of your hiring is still going to come about through standard, straightforward, consistently repeatable recruitment strategies. You need to continually refine your help wanted ads; you need to use high school and college placement offices; you need to develop "bird dogs" in appropriate social service agencies. These are repeatable, ongoing strategies that have proven their value over and over for every type of business.

But sometimes managers just want to have *more fun* with the hiring process than these strategies provide. The new job market allows for—nay, encourages—out-of-the-ordinary approaches to finding the right people. So what can you do? Here are thirty-one different ways to attract more help.

1. Decide to create physical, emotional, and mental tools so that you enjoy being a spontaneous, one-on-one, belly-to-belly recruiting machine.

All the other tips given in this chapter are designed to help you recruit more people, but this first tip is to encourage you to decide you're going to do it—that you're going to enjoy recruiting, enjoy talking to people about your job openings, enjoy networking, enjoying gathering the necessary skills, tools, and techniques to make you a first-rate recruiter. Once you decide you're going to do it, and you're going to enjoy doing it, you're 50 percent of the way home!

Most managers never make this decision. They do the work—developing recruiting brochures and contacting agencies—but only because they have to, because it's part of their job. To make the decision to become a great recruiter, and to enjoy the process, is the most effective tactic you can possibly develop as a manager. When you prepare and train yourself to easily talk to people about coming to work for you, you'll discover that you are naturally running into more and more people to talk to!

The secret is to prepare your tools, so that you don't have to keep reinventing the wheel. That's what the next thirty suggestions are all about.

2. Create a recruiting business card.

You need a simple card the same size as a business card that you can hand out during your day, just as you would a business card. Here's a sample of the front of the card Steve developed for himself and his managers.

> # Subway
>
> *Come Join Our Winning Team!*
> *We're hiring at:_____Phone #:_____*
> *Please Contact:_____*
>
> **See back of card for details.**

On the back of the card, he listed thirteen benefits of coming to work for him, including:

* Free meals
* Paid vacations
* Quarterly evaluations
* Promotion from within

The style of your recruiting card should conform to your particular business, but you'll discover that a card is more direct, more efficient, and more motivating than handing out your business card.

3. Prepare a simple script for yourself to use when handing out your card.

Writing a script for yourself—phrases you could use, questions you could ask, little jokes you could tell—makes it easier for you to talk to likely candidates about coming to work for you. By thinking about what you want to say ahead of time and writing it out, you're more likely to actually do it!

Steve discovered that handing out a recruiting card without having a script to go with it was simply too daunting. It certainly wasn't a campaign that his managers used very often. But once they wrote out scripts with simple sentences and easy phrases that could be memorized and practiced, and that could be used over and over again to break the ice, the managers found the play easy to perform!

The scripts are just what you'd think they are. Very simple, straightforward statements such as, "I'm looking for help. Might you be interested?" Or, "Anybody you know might need fifteen to twenty hours a week of easy work?" Or, "I have a great crew working with me right now. You'd probably fit in well, if you're in the market for a better-paying job." Or simply, "I'm the mellowest manager in the world. Want to come to work for me?" You might say these things anyway, *without* a script. *With* a script, you are more likely to go ahead with it.

Make it easy on yourself, so that you can ask a few quick questions to find out who's interested and who isn't. In fly fishing, it's called "presenting the fly." You want to just float it by a likely person to see if there are nibbles. If not, just move on! You can do this kind of recruiting anywhere, any time. When you've practiced your script, you'll do it without thinking, naturally, without embarrassment. And the crew you assemble this way will be your own crew—handpicked, perfect for your particular team!

4. Pick up "going out of business" employees.

The nature of business is that some are just starting up and some are just going out. It's the ones that are going out that are prime pickings.

For example, one of our local Skippers restaurants made one of those "sudden closings"—here today, gone tonight. The first thing Steve did when he heard this was have his human resources manager call the manager and suggest that she come in for an interview. The manager said thanks. But it was too late. She and her entire crew had been hired by another quick-service food chain. The new company gave the group a package deal.

In another instance, Steve hired a fellow who had been working in a gas-and-convenience shop across the street from one of his stores. Just from outward signs, he could tell that the business was probably close to folding. Steve told the fellow briefly that if for any reason he found himself looking for another job, he should come across the street and talk. Sure enough, within two weeks he was interested. "If you ever get tired of this place," goes another of Steve's scripts, "our business is booming. We're always looking for good help."

5. *Ask your customers to work for you!*

One of Steve's supervisors sometimes encourages his managers to use a script that says, as the customer is being rung up at the cash register, "Would you care for chips, a drink, or a job with that today?" And then give a big grin! Sometimes, it just fits!

Obviously, your repeat customers are the ones who love your place—and love what you're doing and how you're doing it. That's the kind of person you want to work for you!

6. *Use in-house recruiting brochures.*

This is not a new idea. McDonald's, Wendy's, Taco Bell, and most every other franchise use some type of in-house recruiting brochure to interest their customers in becoming employees. An in-house brochure gives your customer a nice advertisement for why it's a good place to work—in much more detail, and in more open communication than you can get with the help wanted ads. Using in-house help wanted brochures is a well-known and widely used tactic because it works!

In Denver, as in most large metropolitan areas, help wanted ads in the major papers are so expensive that a large percent of small businesses are shut out of that avenue. Therefore, these in-house brochures become an efficient form of "street fighting" for these managers. You never know which customer's children or grandchildren might be looking for a job. So let them carry your brochures out into the world!

You can increase the efficiency of these brochures, at the right time, with the right people, simply by asking if they're interested in working as you hand out the brochure. This is what you were advised to do in the previous tip, as well. Obviously, many of these tactics work even better when used in combination. This is a good example. Asking your customers to look at and maybe fill out the application in an in-house brochure will literally double your responses from these brochures. And such asking is made easier when you have written a script!

Of course, you need to do this recruiting in a way that signals to your customer that business is great and that's why you need more good help, rather than "we're hard up and panicking because we can't get anybody to work." It's a fine line. As manager, you will know which of your customers, or which type, are ripe for your approach.

7. Make job applications available.

Often, job applications are part of your recruitment brochure. But if you don't have a brochure, the application itself can be effective. It cuts right to the chase. "Here's an application. Fill it out." It might be helpful to have pens available near the stack of applications. And maybe a sign inviting customers to have a free cup of coffee as they fill out the application.

Granted, having a pile of applications sitting in a conspicuous place will encourage many people to take them who will never fill them out, never bring them back. But paper is cheap, compared to not having enough employees! At certain McDonald's locations they have started putting applications in the carry-out bags! Some locations also have hiring notices on standing cards, table tents, and tray liners. Steve's followed suit in some of his stores, passing out several hundred applications in a week's time. This is a good way to get out the word, and it leads to word-of-mouth advertising.

8. Recruit via direct mail.

Direct mail works especially well if you either have a mailing list, such as for local high school or college students, if that's your target audience, or if there's a particular neighborhood in which you need help. When you're looking for older workers or housewives, the direct mail "coupon" companies can target particular zip codes or areas of influence.

Wendy's has used this approach in many places around the country by including its help wanted advertisement in with neighborhood coupon packages. The average response rate for direct mail advertising is 1 to 3 percent. This means that when an advertiser sends out 1,000 coupons, he can reasonably expect 10 to 30 responses. So if you sent out 1,000 job announcements in a particular area, you might expect to receive anywhere from 10 to 30 responses. The direct-mail help wanted coupon is still a new enough approach that it gets the attention of potential applicants (or their parents or kids).

One of the questions we asked in a survey we conducted regarding recruitment techniques was how entry-wage workers chose which jobs to take. We were surprised to discover that almost half of all applicants surveyed chose their jobs because of location! This is why neighborhood-specific campaigns work as well as they do.

9. Use help-wanted doorhangers.

Similar to direct mail but distributed one on one, these job recruitment notices allow you to target the neighborhoods around locations where you need help. But doorhangers can also be used in-house, at fairs and seminars, around the schools, or wherever else appropriate. Make them bright, noticeable. They can be just $8^1/_2 \times 11$ flyers, or actual doorhangers from the printer, with notches cut to allow hanging on doorknobs.

10. Put up posters and give out flyers.

The difference between posters or flyers and doorhangers is generally only the cut and fold of the paper. Doorhangers are easier to distribute on people's doors in neighborhoods, while posters and flyers are easier to distribute in public places. Help wanted posters and flyers are generally small enough—say, $8^1/_2 \times 11$ inches—to not be obtrusive when you put them up on community bulletin boards in local supermarkets, senior centers, college dormitories, and the like. A flyer is often a time-dated offer, often printed on two sides: now hiring, through August 29. The flyers are handed out or put beneath windshield wipers. A poster, on the other hand, is printed on one side and is generally more ongoing.

Another very direct and very effective way to get more help is to simply bribe your way to a full crew! You can:

11. Pay applicants $25 to fill out an application.

This isn't as crazy as it sounds. Coming in to fill out the application is often the hardest part for some workers. Your offer of money gets them over the hump! Of course, you may want to tie certain limitations to this offer, such as: They are of working age and have a local address. Just make sure your offer is eye-catching and stimulating.

12. Offer a signing bonus.

Young people especially seem to enjoy an offer couched in monetary terms, even if the signing bonus is minimal—anywhere from $15 to $150. Almost everybody today is aware that professional athletes, many of them close to the same age as your applicants, often receive astronomical signing bonuses, with much newspaper publicity. When you offer a signing bonus it puts the new employee in the spotlight, gives him a sense of being in the major leagues, at least for a moment. Again, "just for a moment" is often just enough. Depending on what you're offering, you may want to hold back at least some of your signing bonus for thirty to ninety days.

OK, so now you've bribed them into applying, and bribed them into signing, so the next logical step is to bribe them into staying with you.

13. Offer bonuses to employees who promise to stay on.

You might want to offer a free color television after three months. Why not? You'll be saving that much money and more if the new employees don't quit after thirty to sixty days. Or promise extra pay, special bonuses, or vacations if they stick around a full year. One enterprising retail outlet gives new employees a free weekly car wash for first two months.

But bribing applicants is only one area for bribing.

14. *Bribe your current employees for referrals.*

Your present employees are a primary source for new hiring leads, so make those leads worth money. For example, you can offer your current employees fifty dollars if you hire someone they recommend who sticks around for three months. Or instead of fifty dollars, maybe you want to give them ten free uses of the company car, fifty dollars worth of company products, or personal use of some other company asset that lends prestige, comfort, or entertainment. Bribery, under many different names, is a long-practiced, widely used method of getting and keeping employees, simply because it works.

15. *Register with state and local government employment agencies.*

Suppose your budget just can't handle the added cost of bonuses (bribes) at this time. You want to talk people into coming to work for you, at a straight hourly pay, just because you are a great boss with a great place to work. How do you get a chance to talk them into it? Your local unemployment office generally offers placement services, but if they don't, they know who does.

This may not seem like a guerrilla tactic, but these services are in fact used by so few businesses that they are worth mentioning here. Your results will be best if you go into these offices personally and fill out the necessary forms. Get to know the man or woman who will be sending you applicants. All sorts of people go through these government employment agencies, so let the agencies know exactly the type of person you're looking for. When you make the effort to get to know the people in these agencies, they'll make an effort to get you the right applicants.

16. *File with state and local social service agencies.*

You'll find many of these local agencies at your local courthouse or city building. Or check the telephone book yellow pages for a listing of them, then call to find out what they do and where they're at. From the Social Security Administration, to Rehabilitative Services, to the Welfare Department, to the local youth services bureau, almost every agency has a division designed for employment development of their constituents. As recommended for government employment agencies, go to the agencies' offices and file your applications. When these social service workers meet you, get to know you personally, they are more likely to send you applicants who will truly make a contribution to your organization, rather than an applicant who simply has no other place to turn.

17. *Contact your local probation officer.*

This suggestion is in the same arena as the previous two tips, but deserves its own place because it is so often overlooked and can be very efficient. When you contact the local probation officer, tell her you're looking for the exception to the rule. Many of the kids on probation are truly ready to turn their lives around and prove they are trustworthy, loyal, and dependable. For many employers, the probation department has proven to be a great source of good workers. Obviously, you need to trust your intuition about who to hire and what work to offer. But you need to do this anyway!

18. *Offer free "How to Get a Job" seminars.*

As a manager, you already know what it takes to get a job. You know what you are looking for, and you know what you did to get the various jobs you have held. Write down what you know, and prepare an hour-long presentation. If you leave plenty of room for questions and answers—which is where a lot of the practical information will be offered—you can perform a service for your community and at the same time pick up job applicants for your own business. You might offer these seminars through your local chamber of commerce, youth services bureau, or adult education classes.

19. *Speak to area high schools and colleges.*

At the local schools, you can offer your "How to Get a Job" talk or volunteer to talk about your business, your profession, or the local economy. Sure, almost any manager could do the same thing, but very few managers actually volunteer to do it!

You can expect to receive a minimum of two calls inquiring about employment every time you talk to a high school or college class, although sometimes these calls come six months down the road! Talking to classes is the perfect way to sell your company and convince thirty or forty potential employees that you would make a great boss!

In some instances when you are talking to high school and college students, you may find yourself marketing to the kids of potential employees! ("Any of you kids have moms who are looking for noon-hour work?") Getting out and talking is the key.

20. Talk to older applicants and/or parents of potential employees.

You don't need to limit your talks to just where the applicants might be at that moment. You can also go to where their parents, grandparents, or teachers might be. You can give talks at clubs, churches, and civic groups. It really doesn't matter what your talk is about—whether it's the local economy, your breakthrough industry, the relationships between business and state. Just let it be known that you are available. Any time you're in front of an audience you can always find an appropriate moment to announce that you're looking for help. Are these your prime applicants? Not necessarily, but they might be the parents of potential employees or people who might know someone their own age in need of work.

21. Make friends with high school counselors, teachers, coaches, and principals.

If you haven't already, it's time to make these local contacts. You don't need to give talks. It's perfectly acceptable to just call these people out of the blue and tell them you're looking for help. There's no need to beat around the bush. You'll be surprised at how many of them want to help you, and how soon the referrals will start coming in. These people want to see young people working!

22. Give scholarships.

If you're a little shy about calling cold and asking for favors without giving something in return (other than a job), set up a program that puts some business money aside for student or employee college work or special training, or that in some other way supports an applicant's school experience.

School is where young people spend most of their day. They have athletic fees, uniform costs, and travel expenses, any of which you could find out about and make the object of your program. If your jobs are open to young people, you need to go where they are! Your demonstrated employment abilities and pro-education attitudes will make a difference in the caliber of people brought your way.

23. Use radio commercials to publicize job openings.

Following the principle, "go where the workers congregate," find out which is the most popular radio station in your area. Radio works not only to announce your new products but also the fact that your business is so great you're ready to add a few more players to your team.

If there's a local station kids listen to, that's a good one to use. If there's a station that targets homemakers, and that's whom you're going after, advertise there. This is not a usual advertisement, and it's for this reason that it often gets the listener's attention and gets the job done quickly!

24. Use recorded messages.

If radio advertising is too costly, then you can slant your newspaper advertisements and poster and flyer advertising toward simply getting the applicant to call a recorded message for hiring information. This encourages the person to leave a name and number if he is still interested after listening to your pitch. It also gives the advantage of letting the applicant call at any time of day or night or on weekends. And it is a "baby step" as compared to the "giant step" of applying live.

25. Use wide banners.

For short periods of time many companies drape banners across the front of their stores inviting not only customers but those driving by to inquire about work. The banners might simply say Now Hiring! or Applications Accepted Today! or Job Openings Here Now! The message can be straightforward or clever. They attract much attention and are likely to bring in people who might not otherwise have noticed your business. But you don't want to leave such banners up too long, lest they lose their eye-catching effectiveness.

26. Use airplane advertising.

This takes the banner idea to a new height! Airplane advertising, although expensive, is often comparable to big-city newspaper advertising. The airplane can pull a banner saying, Help Wanted—Apply at Willies Today, and bring it to football games, parades, or special days at the beach. And it's a lot of fun for everybody concerned!

27. Place ads in sections of the newspaper other than the help wanted section.

This tactic works well, especially when there's careful attention to exactly where in the paper the advertisement will appear and on what days. Of course, as mentioned in Chapter 7, you need to track your results to maximize your return.

28. Direct your advertising to special interests.

Advertise for a first baseman, volleyball player, or bowling enthusiast and invite that applicant to try out for the company team—and mention, by the way, that you have to be employed by the company!

For companies that sponsor city leagues and recreational or interdepartment sports teams, this is a clever, eye-catching ad idea that just might bring someone around who otherwise might not consider applying.

29. Run an ongoing "Congratulations" campaign for local achievement.

Find a way to recognize the achievements of local heros and call attention to your business at the same time. Look for people who get their names in the paper for successful accomplishments. You might contact students who earn dean's list or who receive volunteer achievement awards, or those who participate in neighborhood improvement projects.

This is generally a more long-term tactic to fill your business with high achievers, rather than an avenue to fill short-term vacancies. Along with your congratulations, you include a note, a company flyer, and an application, saying something like, "We're always interested in successful people like you."

30. Have a booth at fairs, carnivals, or high school or college events.

At your booth you will be able to hand out applications for job openings and otherwise publicize your business as a good one to work for. This tactic generally requires that you pay a nominal fee to the sponsor of the event. To make the hiring effort more successful, you may need to offer something like a free sandwich or drink, or some other special item to encourage potential employees to fill out applications. Again, this is a way of going to the mountain, when the mountain won't come to you!

31. Hire "survey people" to canvass local students about your company.

Select spirited high school or college students to survey their peers on their attitudes about your business. Then provide the survey takers with bonuses for any names, addresses, and phone numbers of good prospects. Give bigger bonuses for those who are hired.

Obviously, this same survey could be taken in other target populations, such as housewives or seniors. The idea is to talk to more people about your business, and get the names and addresses of those who might be interested in work. By hiring survey takers, you are basically hiring recruiters, which may seem on the edge of professional ethics, but remember that these are tactics for the jungle.

Tactics on the Edge

All of the above tactics are straightforward and aboveboard, and they should generate more than a sufficient number of new applicants from the open market.

Even though you may be able to generate a sufficient number of applicants in these ways, you may discover that your competitors are using other tactics that seem perhaps a bit shady, or at least on the edge of ethical. It's wise to be aware of them, so they are included here.

First, let's have a quick word about some of these tactics, which are targeted at enticing your competitors' employees to come to work for you. Direct wooing of your competitors' employees is somewhat akin to the man who woos another man's wife. He may indeed succeed in getting the lady to switch partners, but then he puts himself in the position of never really trusting her loyalty to him! After all, if she switched once for a better deal, might she not switch again?

Such switching happens all the time in the business world, of course, and the vows we take with our employers are usually not as sacred as those we take with our mates. But when we consciously set out to steal our competitors' helpers, we are heading down a road lined with alligators and swamp rats.

There are higher roads to take. It's best to let your new employees come to you of their own volition, without your having suggested that they break previous commitments or loyalties. With that said, here are a few of the shadier tactics you might want to watch out for.

1. Put your help wanted flyers on the cars of employees in your competitors' parking lots.

A brazen, "let's fight" tactic, the well-placed flyer technique has been used with some short-term success. For this to work, the differences between the working conditions and/or pay scales of the companies have to be significant. Make sure you are not lagging behind your competitors in what you offer your employees or they may come out one day to find such flyers on their cars!

2. Give out "I like the way you work" cards to good employees of competitors.

A formal version of the informal wooing that goes on whenever competitors either openly or secretly visit each other's site, this tactic is also brazen. Unless the employee is feeling disenchanted—-or even if he *is* disenchanted, the first thing he'll probably do with the card is show it to his boss! Be prepared to enjoy confrontation!

3. Use direct mail to interest your competitors' employees.

Find the names and addresses of your competition's managers, and then direct-mail to them at home, offering them a job.

4. When the "big guys" come to town and hire en masse, take flyers to the parking lot and give their prospects a choice.

The big guys—Wal-Mart, Home Depot, and the like—are hiring engines. Their publicity and hiring offers bring in large numbers of applicants, so why shouldn't you grab a little of the action?

We've either experienced some of the other hardball tactics directly (read been on the short end of the tactics) or have had close friends who have suffered from them. We don't enjoy engaging in these tactics and we don't especially enjoy having them done to us. But if truth be told, as far as this tactic is concerned, a raid on the "big guys" might just boost the ego of a small local merchant. Alas, you have a short-term gain at the cost of a long-term weakness.

5. Use bait and switch.

Hire ten people at ten dollars an hour for ten hours a week, and then when that's done, announce that you're going to keep five people for twenty hours at five dollars an hour. This bait-and-switch tactic has been used by at least one national firm.

Seems like the managers are going to a lot of work to create some unhappy people, but it does in fact get workers in the door and gives managers a chance to screen for who works hard and who doesn't.

6. Hire good-looking men and women to interview candidates.

You might say this is another type of bait and switch, where the beautiful recruiters are hired, at a handsome wage, for a couple of weeks, until the crew is put together. "If someone this beautiful has agreed to work here, it must not be all that bad—we want to work here too," goes the applicant's thinking. Welcome to guerrilla hiring! It's often a month or two before they realize the "good looker" is nowhere to be found.

7. Use employees to round up warm bodies.

Send a couple of your local, well-known employees to go cruising for prospects—like old-time sailer conscriptions—around to the high school, the pinball parlors, the city parks, and so on. "Bring 'em back today, alive! Give 'em food, drink, then sign 'em up!"

This is a workable tactic for special occasions, when you need a lot of help quickly, and you find yourself really scraping the bottom of the barrel. You need someone, anyone, right now! Your recruiters pull up to the curb, say something as simple as, "Hey, any of you guys want free food and drink, and to make some money for a couple of hours' work?" This is a short-term, special-occasion tactic, which you'll need to combine with the next tactic.

8. Pay by the day.

This is work today, get paid today! It's a tactic that does not lead to drawing the highest-caliber applicant. But it can also be used in your help wanteds, your doorhangers, and your flyers.

Generally, this tactic is going to draw those applicants who are in more desperate circumstances, and not those with long-term orientations. It's possible, however, to turn these employees into long-term workers by agreeing with them that they'll get paid daily for the first two weeks, and then go on the regular payroll schedule. This helps the employee in strained circumstances to get over the hump and makes the cruising conscription a lot easier!

9. Use TV commercials.

Guerrilla tactics generally imply low-cost, fast-hitting strategies, and clearly television commercials are not low in cost and sometimes take many repetitions before they are effective. And yet, as today's worker shortage continues, these nontraditional avenues for recruitment will become more mainstream, less "fringe" tactics.

With the advent (or more accurately, the roaring presence!) of cable television, with fifty channels or more now available, the cost of TV time is actually coming down, not only on the public-access channels but on most other airwaves (channel waves?). With the development of low-cost video equipment, more companies are producing television commercials, so the production costs for commercials have also come down.

But TV is still a tricky medium. Low-budget commercials are obvious and often embarrassing. Television has the potential of sucking up the majority of your recruitment dollars while giving you a very small return. That's why it's the last one on our list! Enter this arena slowly, carefully—perhaps "sponsoring" local high school or college sports events or special coverage programs. Don't look to TV commercials as a quick fix, but more as an image booster for your other tactics.

★ ★ ★ ★ ★

We present these tactics to give you not only specific ideas for recruiting but also the sense that creative energy is OK—that it is expected, required. Let your mind roam. Give yourself permission to think up wacky and unconventional approaches to attracting job applicants. These original ideas may bring you just the type of crew you enjoy most!

But getting new applicants to apply is only the first step. How do you then convince them that yours is the exactly right place for them to work? How do you reel them in, once they've nibbled at the bait? For answers to these questions, turn to the next chapter.

9

Reeling Them In

It usually takes more than three weeks to prepare a good impromptu speech.

—Mark Twain

A large chunk of your recruitment problem would happily disappear if you were able to capture a larger percentage of those who have come in or called with interest in your job opening. When the applicant comes in or calls, you want to be ready, just as the spider has the web already spun before the fly enters the barn! But you also want to make this new relationship seem friendly, casual, and somewhat impromptu.

Remember, to an applicant the hardest job in the world is looking for a job. So your work as manager is to help your prospective employees enjoy the application process more. In fact, you should help them enjoy it so much that the job hunt gracefully ends for them when they come into your business.

In previous chapters, we've briefly discussed making the application process easier for candidates, but "making it easy" is such an integral part of Reeling Them In, and thus solving your hiring problem, that a closer look is warranted.

Call, Mail, Just Drop By?

Obviously, one of the first steps in screening candidates is in the way you tell them to contact you. Generally the more advanced a position, the more hoops the candidates have to jump through, beginning with the first contact. If you're looking for a special person with special training, and you'll know her when you see her, then you can have applicants send resumes to a post office box number. You can hide behind the screen of anonymity while you privately review the peons at the gate who are clamoring to work for you.

On the other hand, if you're trying to encourage a great many applicants, you'll want to make it easier for them to contact you. By far the easiest way for them, though not necessarily for you, is to have them telephone. The second easiest way for applicants to reach you is for them to come by any day "between the hours of ____ and ____" and fill out an application. Or, applicants can come by on "Tuesday or Wednesday between 2 and 4," and fill out an application. Let's look at the process of welcoming applicants' inquiries.

The Initial Response

Obviously, you're going to generate the most responses to your help wanted ads if you invite people to just call, whenever they happen to read the ad. This makes it easy for them. They're not making a commitment yet, and they can take a "baby step" in your direction, checking you out. On the other hand, telephone responses are a lot of work for you and your staff.

The first step is to determine that you will enjoy this phase of your work. It means talking to many different people, time and again, until you have a full corps of applicants. Let it be fun, and a "team building" experience for all involved!

Next, check your support systems. Many establishments have friendly, interesting help wanted advertisements and brochures, but when the applicant calls he encounters someone on the other end who acts rushed, irritated, or bothered by the call, and simply goes through the mechanics of giving the applicant the necessary information.

If you encourage phone calls, then assign one person—or, if necessary, two—to taking those calls, answering the phone during the time your advertisements are running or your hiring campaign is in high gear.

Make it clear to whoever answers the phone that these calls are *not* interruptions in the normal business and are *not* interfering with that person's regular responsibilities. Rather, these calls are normal and very important business. Answering telephone calls is a significant responsibility. Answering applicants' telephone calls is quite likely even more important than the daily business routine.

Telephone Response Scripts

Prepare a script for answering applicants' initial phone responses. The script is for both your own benefit and the benefit of the caller, because it will make the whole process go more smoothly. Many managers resist the suggestion of using scripts, feeling that such mechanical aids will "impersonalize" the hiring process and somehow interfere with honest communication.

This attitude quite likely comes from receiving too many evening telephone solicitations, These solicitors interrupt your dinner and then so obviously begin reading from a prepared script that leaves no room for the listener to interrupt or get back to his mashed potatoes. The listener usually ends up giving his charge card number or setting an appointment for aluminum siding.

However, when used simply and repeatedly, scripts help both the caller and the screener to communicate more efficiently, more gracefully, more precisely. Scripts help to present the truth in the best light possible. The President of the United States wouldn't think of going to a public presentation without a prepared script. He knows what he's going to say and how he's going to say it. He knows what he might be asked and how he will respond. If using a script is good enough for the prez, it's good enough for us.

A Typical Telephone Script

So here's a sample script to use in responding to a caller inquiry about a job opening. The bracketed numbers correlate with ideas in the script that you will want to develop for your own response, and are explained in the discussion that follows.

> *You:*   Hello, this is [your name]. Thank you for calling Barney's.

Caller:	Yes. I'm calling about the job you have advertised for a. . . .
You:	Yes, thank you for calling **[1]**. Our business is [growing/hopping/exploding] so fast that we need a few more people to help us in keeping up with the demand **[2]**. We have a good time here, and we make some money and all get along well **[3]**. We're setting up appointments for people to come in and talk, see what we have going. By the way, my name is [your name]. I'm the [give title]. Who am I talking with, please? **[4]**.
Caller:	My name is Sam Golden.
You:	Great. Well, [Sam], have you ever done [retail/ fast food/warehousing]? [*or*] What is your current situation? **[5]**
Caller:	[Gives experience]
You:	Good. That sounds interesting. One of the responsibilities for this position is [give brief description of one of the qualifying and/or disqualifying factors—working evenings/working weekends/lifting 50 lbs/knowing computers/being age 21]. Is that a problem for you?
Caller:	No, it is not.
You:	Another thing we're looking for is [supply information]. How do you fit with that?
Caller:	[Gives response]
You:	[If "disqualifying" factors are apparent]: [Sam], we've had very good responses to our ad, and we already do have several people who can meet these needs. I hope you'll keep checking the ads for our future openings **[6]**.
	[Or] [Sam], these qualifications are very important for this job, and rather than hire someone who doesn't have them we'll probably just keep looking until we do find someone. You are wel-

come to come in and fill out an application at your convenience, but I can't be very encouraging about a job, at least not in the next couple of months. I thank you for calling, though, and I'm sure there's something that's going to be just right for you somewhere. You might want to call us back in a couple of months, if you still haven't found anything **[7]**.

[If applicant is still viable, after asking first two qualifying questions]: What kind of hours are you looking for? **[8]**. Great. We'd like to talk with you more. Show you what we have going. See if we have a match for what you need. How's your time here in the next couple of days? We're talking with people [today/tomorrow/Wednesday/this week]. We are planning to make a decision, to have somebody hired by [date] **[9]**. Can we set up a time for you to come in so we can talk? I have a couple of slots open. This afternoon at [time] or tomorrow at [time]. Are either of these good or is there a better time?

Caller: [Response]

You: Great. We'll see you at [time] on [date]. Thanks again for calling. Oh, one last thing **[10]**. What attracted you to the ad? What made you call?

Caller: [Explains]

You: Great, OK. See you on [date].

Why You Say What You Say

The whole purpose of the phone script is to motivate the good candidates to come in and let the poor ones go without much harm (or time). So here are the ten key points to include in your script:

1. You need to thank the person for calling, or be glad that she called. The person is doing you a favor by listening to your pitch. Welcome to the New Century worker!

2. Tell the caller right away why there's a job open. We like to start off by setting the upbeat tone and letting even those who are not qualified know that we are doing well. Don't let them wonder why you need more help.

3. Plant the idea right away that this is a good place to work and that people do get along well and that you are having fun. And the more you say it, the more true it is. So take every chance you have to say it—even fifty times a day to all the new applicants.

4. Mention early in the phone interview that you are setting up appointments, but don't ask for the appointment yet. Let it sink in a bit, let the caller know where this conversation is heading, but you're not sure yet you even want an appointment with this person. And the caller likewise may not be so sure he wants an appointment with you. Then get friendly. Tell the caller your name. Ask for his name. You're opening up dialogue. On your calling sheet, write down the name. If the person doesn't give you a last name, you don't need to ask for it yet. The caller apparently is not comfortable with you yet. Just move on through the script.

5. Ask *two* questions here, "Do you have experience?" and "What's your situation?" Let the caller answer whichever one she wants. These are not really qualifying questions yet; rather, these questions can be answered easily and the answers tell you a little about the caller. By asking these two questions, you invite the caller to tell you what she thinks is best about her background, and also what her current situation is. Asking about the current situation is a beautiful open-ended question that will always give you great insight into your prospect. As the person talks, take notes.

6. Even though you probably put qualifying items into your help wanted ad, you'll still have people call who don't qualify, hoping maybe they can somehow squeak by. It's time to sort them out. Ask the caller directly just one qualifying question at a time. We recommend sticking with your two main qualifying questions, and using three at the most. Ask the questions in a straightforward, simple manner, eliciting a simple yes or no answer.

7. If the applicant is *not* qualified for the job, let the person off easy. Again, this is why a script is so helpful. Remember, even if the caller isn't a viable applicant today, he may be next month or next year, or someone he knows may be. Don't burn your bridges! Write a script that makes it easy for you to let people down softly.

8. "What kind of hours are you looking for" is again an open-ended question that we like to ask because the caller can answer in many different ways. The caller often will use this as an opportunity to tell you what else she has going in her life (take notes) that will impact on the work hours. The caller might tell you which days she wants to work or which times of the day, whether she's looking for full-time or part-time and why. Answering this question will also let you know if the person is wide open. Keep taking notes!

9. It's motivating—for both the applicants and yourself—to let callers know up front how soon you're going to be hiring, even if it is as soon as this afternoon. It gives you each an idea as to how long this dance is going to take. Knowing there's a definite day set for ending the hiring process is somehow clean and fresh.

Try to make setting up the interview seem informal. Let the caller know it's going to be an easy affair, where "we're just talking" to get to know each other. Again, you want to give callers the feeling that they are participating in the decision about their employment—"seeing if we have a match." You also want to make it easy for them by suggesting two different interview times to choose from, as well as an open-ended time suggestion. How they respond to this choice is also somewhat telling. If the caller takes the earliest possible interview you've offered, that's a good sign. Your percentage of no-shows will be a lot lower when you let callers participate in the decision.

10. Investigative journalists often use the "Oh, by the way" trick to get subjects to open up about something they might not otherwise talk candidly about. (The TV police detective, Columbo, does the same thing!) The trick is, after you have everything packed up and you're ready to hang up the phone, you say, "Oh, by the way . . ." and then you ask the question that

you've secretly been dying to ask since the first minute. As you're finishing, the caller starts to relax. It's all over, it's been successful. In this mood, the caller will often tell you things that you might not have been able to have dragged out in a straight face-to-face question.

"What prompted you to respond to the ad?" gives you good feedback about the applicant, as well as a clue as to how your recruitment efforts are paying off. "Man, I'm ready to take any job I can get . . ." lets you know what you're in for. "I liked that you have a retirement plan" is a lot more promising.

Your best applicants will also want to be helpful right from the get-go, letting you know what it is about the ad they like. With this question, you've already started a working relationship!

Jewels and Cash Money: In-Person Applicants

It's wise to have a script prepared for in-person applicants as well, although it would be much more awkward and inappropriate to actually read from a script as you're talking to someone in person. Still, we suggest writing a script and then memorizing at least the key phrases. It's important to know the progression you want the interview to take.

The principles governing walk-in respondents are the same as for phone inquirers. You want to be efficient and communicate clearly, making it easy on both yourself and the applicant. When you work by script, you won't tire so easily and will give each applicant the proper amount of attention.

Prepare for Walk-Ins

If you have an ad running and you know you'll be having applicants coming in, put on extra help during these shifts (if you have them!) so that you have time to take care of each applicant. Make sure your business sparkles, that fresh flowers are on the table (if appropriate), that the windows are washed, and last week's trash has been removed.

Job applicants are like jewels or cash money to your business. When a diamond or ruby presents itself at the counter, why does the manager so often say, "Yeah, take a seat. I'll get to you when I finish taking care of my nickel and dime business." When you have a flesh-and-blood applicant standing at your door, you generally have a higher-caliber, more motivated person than you do with the phone caller. It's an opportunity to screen the applicant and give a first interview. You've just invested a lot of time and money. Don't blow it here at the starting gate!

Nevertheless, exercise caution in hiring an applicant on the spot, although you might give a strong indication that the job will probably be offered. Everyone wants to feel as though he is "a bit above the crowd." To hire someone on a first interview—at the first meeting—gives a wrong first impression about your business, no matter how badly you need somebody.

A Typical Walk-In Encounter

To begin, be happy the applicant has walked in your door. Here's how a typical encounter should proceed.

You: Hi, thanks for coming in. My name's [give name]. I'm the [give title]. And your name?

Applicant: Lisa Gore.

You: Great. Well, [Lisa], as you can see, we've got a good business going here, so I'll be able to talk with you after I finish up here in a minute. It'll save time if, while you're waiting, you could fill out this application. Can I get you a cup of coffee or a soda while you're doing that?

When you return, engage again in brief small talk to reconnect. Then look over the application. Ask questions about the responses. Compliment the applicant about her work history. "That must have been hard," or "That must have been fun," or "How was that?" Get the applicant talking about her previous work—it'll give you a good sense of how she'll be talking about your work here in another year or two!

Although you can take notes during the interview, telling the applicant that it's important because you don't want to forget anything, I suggest that you put down your pen and refrain from taking notes as the applicant talks about her work history. If she sees you taking notes about her previous jobs, she will start to clam up real quick. You can always make some notes after you've concluded the interview.

In talking about the applicant's previous work, you want to create a "just between you and me, what was it like?" atmosphere. In Steve's company, he has a list of questions that his managers ask potential employees to make sure they cover all the bases.

Some Qualifying Questions

After you've talked about previous work and asked the questions you need to ask to fill out your interview form, then you need to give a brief, no-holds-barred commercial for your working environment. Explain what you're doing, how you're doing it, and why you have a job opening right now. Tell the applicant what a great crew you now have. Then ask one or two more of your final qualifying questions. ("Can you really lift fifty pounds, over and over again, eight hours a day?" "Can you work nights?")

If the applicant fails these final qualifying questions, let her know right then, in a way such as this:

> *You:* It sounds like you'd be really great in some other spot. But I was authorized to fill this position only with someone who can [lift fifty pounds/work nights]. Maybe something else might show up in the next month or two. You might want to check back. We'll keep your application on file.

This is when having a script helps you make the rejection smoother for the candidate and for you. With a script, you don't have to keep reinventing the wheel. You may have to reject 60 to

80 percent of the applicants in the first interview. To have a script helps you do that without losing all the energy that rejection inevitably entails. It's hard to reject somebody, even if you're the coldest-hearted S.O.B. on the block. It always takes something out of you. The script will save a lot of wear and tear on the psyche.

Though you may be rejecting a large percentage of walk-in applicants, the chance is high that the right person will come through your door. The interview takes only about twenty minutes when done right, but at the conclusion both parties should feel as though there is now a foundation on which to build a relationship, if that seems desirable.

A Planned Event

Our intent here was not to give you the exact things you should say in an interview. Obviously, you know which subjects you need to cover for your own business. The point is that you can—should—make the walk-in interview a planned event, such that both you and the applicant enjoy the process.

Surprisingly enough, the more you enjoy the interview, the less you'll have to interview! Set the tone for the interview—fun, quick, efficient—from the first step! The applicants who become your employees will know what to expect, and the applicants who don't will turn into your customers—or future employees.

★ ★ ★ ★ ★

OK, now let's take a look at how you train these workers, and then how you get these workers to hang around, once you've got them in the stables.

10

Train or Pain

We first make our habits, and then our habits make us.

—John Dryden

It's possible to summarize in ten words what it takes to overcome today's hiring problems: a happy manager with good hiring skills and great training. You've probably caught on by now that happiness is the basic tool of management, and that it is something that you can train yourself—and your employees—to experience much more often than most workers ordinarily do.

Good training—first in realizing happiness and then in acquiring skills—is truly the essence of good business, and thus the essence of keeping good employees. So much has been written about methods and procedures of training in the tasks of daily management. Steve has written more than 1,000 pages of training materials, and so we won't try to cover all of that subject here. In this chapter we'll devote ourselves to those aspects of training that most directly help diminish today's hiring problems.

The Essence of Business Artistry

We think everyone has the right to take his work—no matter what it is—just as seriously and as intensely as do professional athletes, concert musicians, doctors, lawyers, and corporate executives. That's why we're true believers in ongoing vocational training. We continue to train ourselves in a variety of skills and interests, and take courses whenever we can find classes that might prove valuable to our work.

In Steve's company, he "trains" in our corporate headquarters almost as much as he trains his rookie employees in sandwich making, store maintenance, and upkeep. After all, the sixteenth-century Italian painter Titian completed many of his most famous pieces when he was over ninety years old. Apparently, everything leading up to that was "training!" Nevertheless, this chapter focuses on the training that is mostly conducted in the first thirty days of employment. "As the sapling is bent," goes the old saying, "so grows the tree."

When Does Training Begin?

Training actually begins in the wording, style, and tone of your classified advertisement, or in the style of your guerrilla recruiting that attracts applicants in the first place. Your corporate culture, your daily presentation, is wrapped up and expressed in your recruitment practices.

When the applicant first walks in the door, and is treated with respect and dignity, in an environment of cleanliness and order, with easy-going humility and forthrightness, he is undergoing his first "training." He's starting to learn what will be expected of him. And the opposite is true also. If the applicant, on his first day, is treated with abruptness and superficiality, in an unclean environment where attention to detail is obviously not important, then this applicant is also undergoing an initial "training." He's learning what is acceptable behavior.

One of Steve's former assistant managers decided to invent a short-cut to training. She figured that the easiest approach was simply to hand the new employee the 200-page training manual, give the employee two or three hours to read it and sign it, and then get to work. We wish it could be so simple!

Training Talents

Steve teaches his managers, year after year, that he does *not* consider training to be simply a "necessary evil." He considers training to be the cornerstone of successful daily activity.

What Poor Trainers Can Expect

1. For every hour up front that you scrimp on training a new employee, you can expect to devote two to three hours, minimum, fixing goof-ups down the line.
2. For every one employee you fail to train well, you can expect three to five phone calls at home to fix the problems and uncertainties of these poorly trained employees.
3. You will have two to three times as much product waste with untrained employees.
4. You can expect a two to three times less productive employee, and thus you're going to require more employees to get the same amount of work done, which will cut into your profits.
5. Your stores, areas, or shops are going to be dirtier.
6. You're going to have more accidents or mistakes, leading to possible lawsuits and workers' compensation claims.
7. It's not going to be as much fun to come to work, and the work is going to be harder while you're there, and you're going to be a lot more tired at the end of the day.
8. You're going to have more theft.
9. You're going to experience a lot more turnover.
10. With untrained employees, you're going to be giving less service, and thus your store is going to have lower sales, and thus your own bonuses, your own "piece of the action," are going to be smaller.
11. You're going to find fewer employees as friends—associates, coworkers, people you can talk and laugh with. It's going to be a "you against them" atmosphere.
12. With poorly trained staff to begin with, you're going to continue to have a poorly trained staff in the long run. It's hard to break the pattern once it's established.
13. Your best employees are going to quit. Your crummy employees are going to rule!
14. You're going to work a lot harder than you need to work, for less money.

15. You're going to get into personality conflicts with your employees and with your bosses.
16. You're going to start looking around for other work because this doesn't seem to suit you. The reason it doesn't suit you is that you didn't do the most necessary part of your job: *Train your employees well!*

If you are the trainer, strive to gain a clear picture of what a good trainer is and the benefits of good training. Try to talk clearly, openly, and simply to employees so that there's never any question about what you're saying and what you're meaning. Your own training will filter down to others.

The benefits of being a good trainer are that you:

* Have more productive employees.
* Have happier employees.
* Have lower turnover.
* Enjoy your job more.
* Are less stressful.
* Have better cost controls.
* Have a cleaner store.
* Have less theft.
* Have fewer no-shows and sick days.
* Generate higher sales, better service, with resulting pride in your products.
* Earn more money through bonuses or raises.

A good trainer has the following characteristics:

1. A good trainer will train the *right person for the right job.* This means you don't just take whoever walks in the door. You wait for the right candidate, and you know who that is by your inner sense of knowing. You need to hire not only the right person for the right job, but the right person for the team you already have working.

2. A good trainer is *patient.* She patiently trains the good employees in all areas of responsibility. And then she's also patient with employees who seem to have difficulty "getting it,"

who are slow, perhaps, and without the automatic skills with which some others may be naturally gifted. Such a slow learner will often prove to be the most dedicated, most productive, most reliable of all workers.

A good trainer is patient with all her trainees. No matter what happens, she never loses her joy! When you're enjoying yourself, you automatically have patience. When you're not enjoying yourself, you're automatically impatient!

3. A good trainer is well organized and methodical. He first *tells* the trainee what he's going to learn. Then he *shows* the trainee how it's done, and then he lets the trainee *do* the task himself, while he, the trainer, watches and helps and answers questions. Tell, show, do—that's the key to basic training exercises.

4. The good trainer *gives frequent feedback*, not just every once in a while. This is especially important in the first thirty work hours. Obviously, you don't want to be breathing down their necks, never giving them a chance to goof up or do things in a way that they themselves easily see as wrong, and which they can quickly fix on their own. Frequent feedback is not only feedback about what needs to be corrected but also about what is being done right. Rewarding good behavior creates more of the same.

We learn such behavior early. When Steve's fourteen-month-old son handed his mother a tissue after she had asked him, she enthusiastically thanked him. With such great feedback, the tissues started coming out of the box at the rate of one a second. "Yes! Yes! Yes!" is a great, great, great feedback that everybody understands and enjoys!

5. The good trainer maintains and communicates *high expectations*. The best employees love to have high expectations that are clear and doable with the tools and in the time allotted. In today's tight hiring climate, there is a tendency to lower your expectations for the workers you are hiring and training, out of fear that they might quit. In fact, what you should be doing is escalating your expectations in order to keep their interest and bring out the latent abilities of their coworkers.

Remember, however, that you're only going to frustrate

yourself and your trainees if you have high expectations but you fail to communicate what those expectations are! They must be clear, open, most often quantifiable, and proven to be a standard achievable by most trainees.

6. The good trainer uses the tools he has been given. In other words, he uses the training manuals, the check-off sheets, and the procedures he himself was trained to use. To invent new ways or find short-cuts is, of course, a natural and permissible approach to training—business is made better by such insights and the natural desire to do things more easily.

But these short-cuts—if they truly are helpful and an improvement over the previous methods—can be communicated to those who set up the training in the first place. These people can then make sure that everybody else in the business is aware of such short-cuts, and that everybody is working off the same page.

7. A good trainer devotes all the time necessary up front to get the trainee well trained from the beginning. The temptation is to get the new people on line, in action as fast as possible. This is OK, as long as training continues in steady, consistent fashion. Big chunks of training up front, and then a steady diet of training over the years, lead to well-functioning business.

Training: The First Thirty Hours

The time when your new employee is going to listen most carefully to you, and follow your instructions to the letter, is during the first two to four hours of the job. And the second most attentive time is the first two to four days on the job. That's why it's important to have these first hours carefully planned.

With entry-level workers, the first hours, first days, and first weeks work will most often determine the success or failure (happiness or unhappiness) of the employee's entire job experience. In the quick-service industry, 50 percent of all turnover is within the first thirty days! And of the first thirty days, the first thirty hours generally set the tone for what is to follow. So here are a bundle of tips to make those first thirty hours "shine."

Thirty Tips for Better Training

1. Do something before the employees' arrival on the first day to let them know you were expecting them and are glad to have them on board. Have places, name tags, or uniforms ready for when they show up. But don't put them into uniform yet.

2. If you are the trainer, or manager, have another employee assigned in advance to help take care of the new employees and answer questions when you're not around. Create a buddy system. Let the new employees know there is a buddy assigned to take care of them.

3. Tell the new employees that you know that the first day is the hardest day, and the first week is the hardest week, and so not to worry if things seem hard, confusing, or difficult at first.

4. Tell them, on the first day, within the first hour, that "We all enjoy working here. After you've been here a month, you'll see why." If you can't tell the new employees this, then you shouldn't be training! Find somebody who can tell the new employees that!

5. Give them a quick verbal outline of what they can expect for the next three hours, and for the next three days, and for the next thirty days.

6. Tell them what time they can expect to go home today.

7. Get their initial paperwork taken care of. Have the new employees fill out W-2s, the I-9s, the time cards. Stick with them while they are doing it. Be present so they can ask any questions.

8. Tell them when they will get paid, how much, and what time period the pay will cover.

9. Take some time to figure out what hours they will work over the next week. This is something in the back of every new employee's mind, and unless this question is laid to rest in the beginning, they will have a hard time thinking about what else you are saying.

10. Give them a tour of the whole facility, which gives them the feeling of being part of the team.

11. During the tour, introduce others on the staff according to what they can "help you with." For example, "This is Judy. She can help you with customer service—she's our best!" Use the introductions of new employees as an opportunity to compliment each member of the staff!

12. If possible, after the tour of the facility and after staff introductions are made, issue uniforms if appropriate for your business and let the employees change into them. Then tell them about your uniform policy.

13. Compliment your new employees on their uniforms, and suggest what a convenience it is to have somebody else taking care of the laundry! People always feel a little funny—sometimes excited, sometimes glad, but often nervous and uncertain about this transition into uniform. This is a tender psychological moment. Recognize it and honor the person who is making the transition.

This might be a good time to again congratulate the workers on being selected for the job. And to simultaneously express gratitude for being able to work with people of such obviously high caliber!

14. Issue the employee training manual to each employee. If your initial paperwork is part of the training manual, then remove that paperwork prior to the employee's arrival and put it back in the manual afterwards, if appropriate. A thick training manual can be psychologically and emotionally daunting. You don't want anything to darken the first bright impressions.

15. Give an overview of the full training: what it will entail during the first day, the first week, the first month. Let the new employees know what they will be able to accomplish after the first month. Tell them now what tasks after training will seem easy and what tasks will be routine.

16. Explain about the company history and philosophy—where it has been, where it is going, how it does business. It's often more appropriate to give this information after the employees know where they will be in thirty days. From their perspective, they can then extrapolate to the larger picture.

17. Give the new employees a bathroom break or a water drink break. By this time, they should have their foot in the door.

You want to go easy, break them in gently. Give them some time to absorb what has happened and relax a bit—out of your presence—before the next phase of training.

18. After the break, give a run-down of company rules and policies. Let them know the "one strike and you're out" events (that is, stealing, drug abuse, customer confrontations). Let them know the policies on being late, on calling in sick, and so on.

If your company has a rules and policies sheet that employees are expected to sign, this is the time to do it. Don't belabor this point, however. In fact, minimize it. "We don't expect any problems. We actually haven't had many problems at all along these lines." In past generations, company policies and regulations have for the most part been simply assumed as understood, taken in by osmosis. Now it is necessary to spell everything out. But they need not be belabored.

Depending on your company, and how long you expect your new hire to work on the first day, this may be the point at which you decide enough is enough and you're ready to end day 1. A case can be made for either going easy or getting to it all on the first day.

19. When you are ready, begin actual physical training. This is the time to give them a chance to get their bodies moving, their hands involved. To review, the three basic mechanisms of training are tell, show, and do. You *tell* them what the task is, then you *show* them how to do it, and then you let them *do* it themselves! And then you tell them again, show them again, and let them do it again. (And then you tell them again, show them again, let them do it again!) And then you tell them what a great job they did and start all over again.

In our company we expect one-on-one training for a minimum of thirty hours. And we expect our managers or certified trainers to conduct this training. We don't want it to be left to "whoever's handy." Training is too important to leave it to chance!

20. After the first training session, show them how you are checking off the tasks learned during this first training session on their training chart. In one toy store in Colorado, new employees have a training manual divided into sections for each of

the major activities for which they will be trained. Under the section labeled, "Opening the Store," fifty different items are cataloged. "Ordering" is another section, and "Cleaning," "Customer Services," and "Closing the Store," each with from twenty-five to seventy-five items, are also listed. Beside each item are check blanks to show whether or not the trainee has been trained in this item. When the trainees see that this is not a haphazard affair but rather a conscious, thought-out process that they are proceeding through on a systematic basis, they are much more likely to give the training credence and respect. And they are more likely to feel a sense of genuine accomplishment when the training is completed (see Chapter 4).

21. Show trainees where the tasks they have just learned are located in the training manual. It is well for the trainer to connect the physical works with the written words, so that the trainee can see how they are linked.

22. Assign buddies or other coworkers to accompany new trainees on their lunch break, if the first shift is an eight-hour one, or on coffee break, if the first shift is only part-time. Whenever possible, the buddy should be someone other than the trainer. But again, attention should be given to the new employees to make sure their first day is warm and welcoming. The buddies assigned to your new employees should ask how it's going, are there any questions or worries that the new trainee has so far.

23. Resume the training. A new task or series of tasks can now be approached different from the first session's training tasks. Such variety will help maintain interest and attention. Again, follow the tell, show, do rules!

24. Prior to quitting time, the trainees should be transferred, whenever possible, back to the first task learned. Or revert to the easiest, most enjoyable task. The point is to find the task that provides an upbeat, successful ending to the first day.

25. Prior to the trainees' departure, ask for a quick review and any comments or questions about their first day's work. This is the time for listening, reassuring, and acknowledging feelings, doubts, or worries. Stop your instruction for a moment

and let the employees vent any feelings. Assure them that their feelings are normal.

26. Prior to the arrival of the new employees on their second day, do something—anything—to let the trainees know that they are expected, they are part of the team, and the company is grateful for their being there. Clean out some lockers or shelves for them to use if you haven't already done so. Or give them special coffee mugs or something for their desks. Let them know you've been thinking about them when they haven't been around.

27. Some time during training on the second day, have the company president, regional manager, or someone else who is away from the job site call the trainees and personally welcome them on board. You might want to send welcome cards, signed by the entire corporate staff, at the end of their first week, as a little thank-you.

28. When possible, assign someone other than the trainer and someone other than the buddy to catch the new trainees doing something good, something right. Let them tell the new trainees what it was that they did well, and assure them that they are doing an OK job and that's all going to work out well.

It's helpful to everybody on your staff when new trainees are trained well. This is a good time to remind the crew of the benefits to them when the new trainees are trained well.

29. Included with the first paycheck should be another "Welcome Aboard" note from the owner or president, or—at the very least—a vice-president or regional manager. It should, when possible, be a note from someone with an impressive title.

The first paycheck is often either an exhilarating or a disappointing occasion for trainees. A note from a Top Banana helps to move it into a positive light and connects the employees with something larger that allows them to start connecting with that which will sustain them over a longer period of time. You, as the manager, may also want to include a note just saying "Thanks, we're glad you're here."

30. Some time during those first thirty hours, "dip" the new trainees lightly and quickly into the dirtiest, most stressful,

or most difficult part of the business. And at the end, have the crew and managers congratulate the trainees on passing the test.

Your most stressful time might be the lunch-hour rush and the most unpleasant task is probably cleaning the bathrooms. Trainees do have to assume these responsibilities at some point. Their initiation into your busiest shift deserves to be recognized, as does their first cleaning of the bathrooms. We've been known to organize a surprise applause when the new trainee has come out of the bathrooms, mop in hand, after completing his first solo bathroom duty. It's nice to be recognized for doing the dirty work.

The "Hiding in Egypt" Principle

Just how valuable is a new employee? The new employee is so valuable that we can take a tip from the scriptures. After Jesus was born, his parents were instructed by the wise men and prophets to take him into Egypt. They hid him there and let him grow to maturity, for the forces of the time were out to get him. In the same way, it's wise to "hide" your new employees, at least for a time. Protect them from the full force of the adversaries. You should let your employees grow strong and secure before you expect them to "be about the Father's business."

"My time is not yet come," Jesus said to Mary, when she asked him to turn the water into wine. So, too, let's not be too quick to ask that of our employees. Sure, they need to be initiated into the trials that are to come, but let them first grow strong with your happy attentions. Only then will you be able to cut your business's turnover rate for the first thirty days.

★ ★ ★ ★ ★

OK, the new employees have survived the first thirty days. And then sixty days. They're on their way. Keeping your employees around is by far the easiest way to shrink your hiring problem out of existence. Tips on how to keep your employees with you longer are what we look at in the next chapter.

11

Retaining Employees

The act of becoming a member [of a corporation] is something more than a contract. It is entering into a complex and abiding relationship.

—Oliver Wendell Holmes, Jr.,
former U.S. Supreme Court Justice

Outside of joy, if there is one single key, one area to focus on, for increased profits and steady growth in this era of worker shortage, that key has to be decreasing your turnover rate. The easiest way to reduce the number of people you have to hire is to reduce the number of people you lose.

This chapter is about retaining those employees. We'll give you some solid ideas for holding on to those hard-sought hourly workers.

Stick With Me, You'll Wear Diamonds!

Steve tells this story about a childhood event that became a meaningful memory:

> When I was a young kid on vacation, a friend of my uncle's took my sister and me out on the town, first to dinner, and then to a carnival, and then for ice cream. He was maybe a little bit tipped when he got there, and a bit more as the evening wore on, but all the time he kept telling my sister and me, "Stick with me, and you'll wear diamonds."
>
> As a kid, I'd never thought about wearing diamonds, how that might be a desirable thing to do. But the way he

said it, clearly it was what we should strive for. OK, we'll stick with you. But I don't think we ever saw him again. He didn't give us a chance to stick with him and wear diamonds. What did stick with me, however, was the phrase and the idea that some people were on the road to high adventure and great rewards. You could go along and have the adventure, and reap the rewards with them!

In his book *Generation X*, Douglas Coupland talks about a "McJob," which he defines as a "a throw-away job which you pick up for a little while and then discard." With the hiring situation the way it is today, such views of the job world are not as unreasonable as employers might hope. For instance, Steve once fired a young man for pilfering from the cash register, which Steve naturally considers to be a fairly basic flaw in employer-employee relations.

The kid went right across the street and got a job at McDonald's. McDonald's didn't call for a reference. They didn't ask why he'd left. Apparently, they were so desperate for help they didn't care (or maybe they assumed that even though he would steal from Subway, surely he wouldn't steal from them).

Most kids don't steal. Most employees are honest. Which means their own opportunities for moving from one job to another are even greater. When the owner of a business is on the premises, and the business is small, the turnover rate is generally low. And yet turnover rates are appallingly high in almost all sectors of business. It's especially high for workers at the entry level. This group is virtually a mobile workforce, moving from one job to another in a single town as easily as some migrant laborers move from crop to crop as the seasons change.

Today there's much less "sticking with the company" in order to eventually wear diamonds. Employees seldom stay long enough to gain the depth and breadth of experience that can take them to greater heights, let alone earn the money to buy those diamonds.

The Cost of *Not* Retaining Employees

Many business owners and managers have never figured out their actual costs for hiring and training new employees. As we explained in Chapters 2 and 4, these figures are essential for putting together an accurate People Plan. Once you know those figures, you will quickly see why improving your retention rate is the surest route to improved profits and return on investment.

Here's a practical, though somewhat generic, checklist for calculating your actual out-of-pocket costs of hiring. It may take you fifteen or twenty minutes, at the very most, to go through this checklist and put in your figures—or at least figures that you know for sure are in the ballpark. With these figures, your whole view of hiring will change.

1. Manager's time in writing ad:
   ____hrs. × __($)__hr. = _____
2. Manager's time in placing ad:
   ____hrs. × __($)__hr. = _____
3. Cost of ad: = _____
4. Estimated hrs. in responding to first inquiries, either over the phone or in person: ____hrs. × __($)__hr. = _____
5. Manager's time in sorting applications and contacting best applicants for first interview:
   ____hrs. × __($)__hr. = _____
6. Manager's time in interviewing:
   ____hrs. × __($)__hr. = _____
7. Manager's time in reviewing applicants, checking references, deciding on which to hire:
   ____hrs. × __($)__hr. = _____
8. Manager's time for introductory hiring session, setting schedule, arranging uniforms, providing training manuals, doing hiring paperwork before trainee is on payroll:
   ____hrs. × __($)__hr. = _____
9. Manager's first hrs. of training:
   ____hrs. × __($)__hr. = _____
10. Trainee's first hrs. of training:
    ____hrs. × __($)__hr. = _____
11. Estimated hrs. of coworkers' helping out trainee with informal training: ____hrs. × __($)__hr. = _____
12. Trainee's first 30 hrs. on job:
    ____hrs. × __($)__hr. = _____

13. Manager's secondary hrs. of training:

____hrs. × __($)__hr. = _____

14. Estimated hrs. for office staff to process and integrate new hire into payroll, insurance:

____hrs. × __($)__hr. = _____

15. Cost of training and introductory materials: = _____
16. Cost of uniforms: = _____

Total Actual Costs: _____

In addition to these actual out-of-pocket costs, there are intangible costs, such as the slowdown in operations caused by new trainees, the loss of management oversight and control of regular crew when management is involved with training, and what economists call the cost of opportunity. This opportunity cost is the cost to the company of the things that the manager is *not* doing when she is spending her time with the "opportunity" for hiring and training new employees.

These intangible costs also include the cost to the business of giving poor service, of having a stressed staff, of having a dirtier store, lower-quality display and merchandising, and, as occurs more regularly with high turnover, employee theft.

Every manager might not be out-of-pocket for every one of the sixteen points above. The manager who operates one store of one business and is on the premises all the time may be able to cut his costs somewhat. And yet, all of these costs—and you may be able to figure others not listed here—are actual expenditures for hiring a new employee. We included number 12—the employee's first thirty hours of work—because generally it takes at least that long for an employee to start being productive—that is, to earn back for the business each hour what he is costing the business.

When you add up the wages for the new worker and for those involved with hiring and training the new worker, don't neglect to include your contributions to FICA, workers' compensation, company insurance if you have it, and other hidden expenses for each new employee.

The Numbers Tell It All

Fifty percent of all turnover in entry-level work occurs within the first thirty days. In Steve's company, he estimates that the total expense for an employee who leaves after a month is $520. That means, if he could tell who was going to leave after a month, he could just hand them $250 on the first day and tell them not to come back, and he'd still be $270 ahead! The corporate offices of Burger King estimate that it costs their company over $1,000 for every employee who leaves at the thirty-day mark. (This is one of the reasons, in Steve's company, he sends a "welcome aboard" card and other "glad to have you" reminders in the first thirty days.)

The interesting thing about these startup costs for new employees is that a break-even doesn't occur until after the second or third month. After the fourth or fifth month, it's a profitable venture. Keeping an employee into the sixth, seventh, and eighth month begins to show up directly at the bottom line!

It may seem incongruous—and a bit insensitive—to be talking about the profit associated with keeping an entry-level employee an extra month or two. But in fact it is this extra month or two from your lower-wage workers, multiplied over many workers, many months, and many stores, that translates directly to the difference between profit and loss.

As every small business owner knows, the cost of labor is consistently and unremittingly one of your highest expenses. And the cost of the first sixty days of labor is generally the highest cost arena of all labor costs. So it's like giving your first-round draft pick a $3 million signing bonus. If he breaks his leg in the first game, arrrgggh!

That's the same thing as happens when your new employees quit after the first thirty or sixty days. For example, if you can extend your average employee's length of stay from 5.2 months to just 7 months—only another six to seven weeks—your annual turnover ratio will drop from 230 to 150 percent. That's more than a 33 percent improvement. That will show up clearly in your profit-and-loss statement.

Why New Employees Leave

A survey by Robert Half International, a Menlo Park, California, staffing services company, found that the most common reason that employees leave is because of "limited recognition and praise." People like to—need to—feel recognized for the work they do, both individually and as a team.

McDonald's was voted one of the top five employers in the country because it excels at giving praise and recognition! The companies that have the lowest turnover rates are those in which recognition and praise are not accidental and arbitrary occurrences but rather are planned, quiet institutions. Managers are required to look for good performance and steady performers who can be recognized and praised. This is the "customer comes second" mentality.

Who has done something right? Who wins the Best Customer Service award this quarter? Who has made the most advancement? Who is the most helpful to other employees? Who has saved the company the most money? Who has been most punctual? Who has been most flexible? Surveys find that it doesn't necessarily take a lot of recognition and praise. In fact, too much too often will dilute the effects. "The prime occupational hazard of the manager," says Henry Mintzberg, of McGill University School of Management, "is superficiality." You want to make your praise honest, deserved, genuine.

George Burns, the legendary comedian, talked about the necessity of honesty in show business, as well as every other type of business. "Honesty is the key," he said. "If you can fake that, all else is gravy."

He was kidding, of course. His humor was honest, his voice was honest, his eyes were honest. He didn't need to fake it. You don't, either. And it's the same with appreciation and recognition. It can't be a spur-of-the-moment, "oh yeah, I'm supposed to appreciate these guys" thing. You have to give real time to thinking about it, to looking and listening and coming up with appropriate, genuine responses when somebody does something well. And as you do this, your coworkers will take a cue and add their own praise and encouragement.

When you must point out negatives to your employees, and discuss behaviors that they must change, make sure that some time within the next week you make the effort to mention at least three things that your employee is doing right!

And in what form should this praise and recognition come?

This is like asking what form flowers should come in. The more varied and colorful, the better! The point here is not how to reward, but rather that you must begin looking at those areas of your business that you want to reward, that you know are important, and then begin looking for employees who are doing those things well.

Get in the habit every day of praising people, thanking them, acknowledging them for doing things well. (If someone isn't doing at least something right every day, that might be a sign.) Typically employees perform approximately 95 percent of their responsibilities in a correct or appropriate manner. And yet, typically 70 to 80 percent of the feedback they receive is negative. Giving negative feedback is easy, even lazy, because it's always obvious when something is wrong. It doesn't take a brilliant manager to give negative feedback. It takes an insightful (joyous!) manager to be able to offer feedback that makes the smooth operation go even more smoothly!

The Three Rs

Jim Sullivan, president of Pencom, Inc., a consulting firm that also operates five high-volume restaurants, suggests that what employees need to have, in order to stick around, are the "Three Rs"—Respect, Recognition, and Rewards.

Respect is an everyday, all-day thing, says Sullivan. "The way you treat your employees," he adds, "is how they'll treat your customers. [The restaurant industry] asks its employees to know the customers' names, what they like to eat and drink. But how many of us know our employees; what their dreams are, what's going on in their families?" If we don't, he says, it's time we do. Today's workforce is composed of human beings, not machines.

And recognition, Sullivan suggests, is something we take time out of our schedule to provide, rather than just something we do in passing. "Remember this," he says, "a pat on the back is only a few vertebra up from a kick in the ass. A pat will take you a lot further than a kick. But it has to be a substantial pat, one that involves taking the time to give your employees the tools and training they need to do the job correctly."

Sullivan agrees that rewards need not be extravagant. A lottery ticket, he suggests, or a note pinned to a time card is sufficient, for "small sacrifices" the employees have made. Larger rewards need to accompany larger contributions. Sullivan agrees with the basic theme: "If they are happy," he says, "they are less likely to quit."

Twenty Ways to Greater Employee Retention

"I am naturally happy," says Dr. Christian Almayrac, the French physician quoted at length in Chapter 3. "Everybody is naturally happy. We can choose to enjoy that happiness, or choose to ignore it. Either way, our nature is joy."

So, what can you do to help your employees enjoy themselves more? Here are twenty suggestions to improve employee retention, which form the basics for job satisfaction.

1. Hire the right person for the job.

Choosing the right person makes everything so much easier. If you hire someone who is not suited for the position, it is only a matter of time before the ax must fall. And the longer that time extends, the more problems will occur. Get the right person first!

2. Communicate openly with your employees.

The more you enjoy your work, the more likely you are to communicate openly and honestly with those around you. It also helps to have built-in forms for communication: quarterly evaluations, newsletters, weekly updates. Yet the basic form of communication is almost always nonverbal communication, in which your own joy of working is communicated in all that you do. For example, Outback, a successful chain of steakhouses, doesn't use written evaluations of their employees. The company expects its managers to communicate with the staff at the beginning and end of each shift with a face-to-face meeting. Let people know what's happening. Communication is more than just "extra paperwork." By communicating well, you avoid the surprises, have more consistency, and experience less frustration. Avoiding the surprises, you create profits.

3. Give recognition for a job well done.

The people who work for you want to be "caught" doing something right! And they want to be recognized when they've put in a long week or month. They want to be recognized for doing so much work without recognition. If we don't recognize the value of our employees, someone else soon will!

4. Stand behind the company.

In some circles it's chic to cut down the employer, no matter who the employer is. Don't fall for it. If the employer had the insight and intelligence to hire you, and you have the honesty and intelligence to stick with the employer, then obviously you are both getting something out of your relationship.

5. Develop your own happy management style.

The manager's attitude is the number one reason employees enjoy their jobs. The manager sets the tone for the whole business. So enjoy your work!

6. Treat everybody equally and consistently.

When it comes to showing your happiness, don't show favoritism. The dishwasher and the man who owns sixteen shopping malls both deserve your full honesty, your full respect, your full attention. Everybody deserves the best you have!

7. Listen and then implement your changes.

Nobody likes to work for a place where his input is not sought, or is ignored, or simply makes no difference. Whenever somebody is talking, the person is giving you feedback, in one form or another, about the business. Listen, and be willing to take suggestions and then implement those suggestions if they are good ones.

8. Reward longevity.

Since, as we've already shown, the longer an employee stays with the company the more profitable she becomes, it only makes sense to reward longevity. Our employees receive an anniversary card on each of their anniversaries with the store, signed by the corporate office staff. After their first year they get a paid vacation, and a substantial pay increase, an invitation to our special Christmas party, recognition in our newsletter, a new colored uniform shirt, a pin showing their years of service, and an invitation to attend a special employee appreciation picnic. Are they worth it? You bet! How valuable are your long-term employees? Have you been showing it?

9. Educate and challenge your employees.

"The art of governing," said Napoleon, "is not allowing men to grow old in their jobs." Every worker—consciously or subconsciously—wants to grow, to be challenged (even if only in figuring out how to make the job easier). Those jobs that continue to provide new experiences, new heights to climb, new arenas to master, are those jobs that will keep the worker around.

10. Focus on retaining managers and assistant managers.

When you lose a manager, you often soon lose 50 to 75 percent of the employees who were hired by that manager, or who were supervised by that manager. Much of the loss comes with the transition to a new manager. The old employees are easily disenchanted by the different rules, standards, and expectations that a new manager brings.

11. Provide fair, competitive compensation.

This is your hook, allowing you to be competitive. Unless you are offering the position of movie reviewer for the local video store, towel clerk for the nudist club, or some equally tantalizing position, you need to be competitive in the wages you pay.

12. Provide strong, positive leadership and direction.

"Where there is no vision," say Proverbs 29:18, "the people perish." Your worker wants to feel as if she is heading somewhere worthwhile, doing something worthwhile to get there, and being of genuine service while moving in a clear direction. "Stick with me, and you'll be wearing diamonds." The lack of leadership is simply a lack of joy in the job, a failure to provide a sufficient number of "thoughts to enjoy" that make the place dynamic. Most people want guidance and direction—a captain to lead them to a worthy destination, which the captain himself also desires.

13. Provide strong and ongoing training.

The lack of creative training is probably the leading factor in 50 percent of the turnover in the first thirty days of employment. All employees deserve the opportunity of good training, just as every child deserves the opportunity of good schooling. So train your employees completely and perpetually! Without such training they are less than they might be, encountering hurdles they need not encounter, carrying baggage that slows them down. Time and again I see employees get reprimands for areas that they were either never trained in or not trained in thoroughly enough. This lack of training, and the frustration it engenders, has a direct link to your turnover rate.

14. Let employees feel they are an important part of the company.

In previous decades, an employee was often "kept in line" by the manager's suggesting, openly or subtly, that the employee was expendable. Sure, it works, for a bit. But it's a shallow, short-term, unhappy management strategy. Today's employees are not easily bullied by the threats of firing. They know other work is available to them.

15. Expect only the best from your employees—and let them know your expectations.

When you communicate high standards, and give your people the tools to meet such standards, you're building the business on a solid foundation. Your best employees excel under such standards. They want and need high expectations to hold their interest.

16. Don't overpromise and underdeliver.

If you're not sure of something—some reward, some promotion, or perhaps a work schedule—suggest it as possibility, rather than imply its certainty. The character Don Corleone, in Mario Puzo's *The Godfather*, suggests that you "let your enemies overestimate your virtues, and your friends underestimate your strengths."

17. Promote from within and make that fact known.

People like to see what's up ahead. They like to know the advancement potentials of their current good work. In our company we have developed a formal training program for crew employees interested in becoming managers, or just growing within the company. We are less and less believers in competition amongst the ranks. When you reduce the competition for management slots, it is important for all the workers to know that your business is strong and growing such that all who deserve promotion will be promoted, one way or another, sooner or later.

18. Provide immediate feedback and positive reinforcement.

When Steve was a young college student, he had a job in the auto department of a discount chain store. He says: "I had worked there, fairly successfully I thought, for about six months when the boss called me in one day and said they had decided to fire me the day before, but now they were going to give me a raise and a promotion to see if I worked out better. I was in shock. I had no idea why they wanted to fire me nor did I have any idea why they wanted to promote me! I was getting *no* feedback!"

Genuine feedback is a necessary support for every employee. Such feedback is resisted only if given with an, "I'm OK, you're a slug," attitude. Again, keeping your joy is the key, where it's obvious that your own happiness, balance, and sense of well-being are *not* at stake when you are giving corrective advice and instructions. When you give feedback in this way, your employee's own happiness and well-being are likewise not diminished. Such graceful (happy) giving of feedback is an art, worthy of a lifelong study! At its best, it comes out, "Here's how you can enjoy this job more. . . ."

19. Fire employees when necessary.

No one wants to work with a jerk, a sexist, a know-it-all, or someone who talks on the phone to her boyfriend while you do the dirty work. You're going to lose your good people if you don't get rid of your bad ones!

20. Keep a green and clean environment.

Have you created an environment that your employees enjoy coming to work in? You need to keep your place clean. And you need to continually upgrade your tools, policies, and procedures for cleanliness. These policies and procedures for keeping a green and clean environment are sometimes the policies that are, at first, most resisted or most neglected. On the surface they don't seem to directly influence getting the job done, serving the customers, or getting the product out. But people deserve to work in clean environments, and they will consistently work better, longer, and harder in such an atmosphere.

Contrary to news media suggestions, most of the oldest and most successful companies have consistently established traditions of cleanliness and doing the job right. No company intentionally sets out to spoil its nest. What is right in one generation becomes obsolete in the next generation. But the best companies—the most profitable businesses—always work to stay on the leading edge in maintaining a green environment for their employees, for their customers, and for their communities.

★ ★ ★ ★ ★

By following these twenty basic guidelines, your employees are going to stick around longer. How do you make sure they're staying on the straight and narrow? You review their work, of course. Turn to the next chapter for a review of reviewing.

12

Let's Review
Your Work

Feedback is the breakfast of champions.
—Ken Blanchard and Spencer Johnson,
The One-Minute Manager

On the voyage to the moon, the *Apollo* spaceship was technically off course more than 90 percent of the time. Small corrections were consistently needed to return the ship to the plotted course and achieve the objective. Such course corrections were expected and planned for. The same holds true in business.

Obviously, we give each other informal feedback every day, both overtly and covertly. We communicate with each other, directly and indirectly, making corrections as we go, just like the *Apollo* spaceship, on our way to a successful day. This ongoing performance review is already part of everybody's ordinary work climate.

But to fine-tune your work, to take it to the next level and to make the business more productive, you can formalize this review process, with the result that you are happier with your employees and your employees are happier with you and their jobs.

Job Happiness Is Key to Productivity

As you've learned by now, enjoyment of the job is the highest priority, and thus it is also the primary reason for the performance review. With such joy comes higher efficiency and higher productivity. As an example of how the performance review increases job enjoyment, consider this.

Steve plays a lot of golf. Obviously, every time he hits the ball, he gets immediate feedback on his performance: He knows if he pulled or hit it straight on, too hard or too soft. By playing golf every day, he gets better. He's getting feedback from his own performance.

But sometimes he plays with the course pro or some other highly skilled player. And he asks for more formal feedback. When he does, his game improves much more rapidly. And then sometimes he has his golf swing videotaped. Again, he has doubled and sometimes quadrupled the amount of helpful feedback available to him. His game improves that much more, and because he loves golf, he enjoys himself even more.

The same holds true for most other sports. That's why professional football teams always spend the day after the game reviewing films. Sure, if you've missed a tackle you know it immediately. And if you miss a block you know it right away, right then. If the opposing receiver gets behind you and catches a winning pass, you know it. You have immediate feedback.

Yet the films allow you to see exactly how that receiver made the move on you. You can see how he faked you out. You took a step to the left when he moved his head to the left. But he moved his head to the left, and took a step to the right.

Professional baseball player Tony Gwynn, of the San Diego Padres, is one of that sport's most avid students of game films. He spends hours studying his batting rhythms and many more hours studying the pitchers he will face. It isn't a coincidence that he has won six batting titles thus far in his career.

The Value of Regular Feedback

Regular feedback is the heart of a job performance program. Michael Jackson, the dynamic founder of Career Track, a management consulting firm, suggests seven primary payoffs to a good job performance program.

1. *Evaluations bring out the best in people.* The difference between a champion swimmer and someone who simply likes to swim is that the champion has constant feedback by the numbers. He knows where he's at and where he needs to go.

2. *Evaluations identify under- and overperformers.* In the rush of the day you may assume that you can sense who is working and who isn't. However, with formal evaluations that have specific criteria for acceptable performance, you often discover that the surface picture is not always accurate. Evaluations help you remain accurate.

3. *Evaluations protect your organization legally.* One of the most common lawsuits brought against employers is for unlawful termination. Regular, honest, upfront evaluations make such lawsuits both less likely and less successful.

4. *Evaluations set the directions for next review period.* To formalize your training and professional growth, you need to know what you're shooting for and how to aim for it. Evaluations play a major role in actualizing your quarterly growth potential.

5. *Evaluations signal that you care.* To keep your employees interested in their job, you have to keep interested in them. By paying attention to their job skills and progress, you are signaling that you know they are part of the team and that their input matters.

6. *Performing evaluations helps develop you as a business leader.* This feedback we are talking about here is found at every level in every business. As you hone your own skills in giving performance appraisals, you are honing your business acumen. These skills will help you wherever you go in your career.

7. *Performing evaluations helps reduce turnover.* This is true for both short- and long-term employees. Employees like to know how they are doing, and feel strangled when they don't know how they're doing. Knowing that an honest, accurate appraisal of their work is coming up (and not just a perfunctory filling out of paperwork) helps employees focus on the job and see what it is they like and dislike, as well as helps them to work to improve. With so much time spent at work, nobody likes to feel that it

simply doesn't matter how well or how poorly they do their job or that nobody else is aware of how the job is being done. Job evaluations help connect employees to a more meaningful job experience, which is what keeps turnover low.

When done right—not intimidating or as threat or as a hurdle they have to surpass, but rather as a means and an end toward greater enjoyment on the job—the performance review can be a central tool in navigating the business ship to successful new ports.

Trimming the Sails

At one time when Steve's company was experiencing very rapid growth, he hired an executive manager to oversee the daily operations of his existing stores while he focused on building and consolidating new outlets. After approximately a year and a half, his turnover rate had more than doubled. And he and his new manager were not happy about each other. So they came to a parting of the ways.

Steve was then faced with the challenge of bringing the turnover rate back down to where it had been before he had delegated his day-to-day responsibilities. He felt that he really did not know his employees as well as he wanted, nor did they know each other. So the first thing he did— which proved to be the most powerful tool he could have invented—was to implement formal "by the numbers" quarterly performance reviews for every worker, from top to bottom. Within the year, his turnover rate had plummeted, and corporate morale had skyrocketed. Steve attributes 60 to 70 percent of this turnaround to the reimplementation of regular evaluations, which are a part of regular communication and feedback.

The Weaknesses in Traditional Evaluation Programs

Sure, suggesting that you have regular performance reviews is far from a novel idea. Many companies have performance reviews, but their turnover remains high. Clearly there are flaws in their review systems, and the following just might be some of those flaws.

No Advance Warning

Almost everyone has had one of those dreams where you're back in school and you're supposed to take a test in a class that you forgot you had even signed up for. What makes such dreams so uncomfortable is the feeling that it's test time, and you have absolutely no clue what this is all about.

In the past, many performance reviews have been exactly like this. It's important to communicate to the new employees, up front, that work reviews are standard in the business. Tell them when their first review will take place and what exactly will be reviewed. If possible, let them see—and take home—a sample evaluation sheet. Include a copy of that evaluation sheet in your hiring packet so that new employees can know what it is you'll be looking for.

Is this like giving the students a copy of the test ahead of time? Sure it is! You want everybody on your team to get A's! That's what being a good manager is all about. It's your job to prepare your employees to sail through their performance reviews. Start by letting them know what's in store.

Unclear or Misdirected Purpose

In the past, much of the evaluation procedure was, either overtly or covertly, directed at establishing whether or not the employee got to keep his job or received a raise or promotion. These reasons are still widely used to justify performance reviews, and under such circumstances it is no wonder that both employee and manager feel stressed at the prospect of such reviews.

In today's competitive work environment, the primary purpose of the performance review is to make sure the employee knows what he is doing and where he is going, and that he is happy to be doing his job.

A One-Way Evaluation

The best way to make performance reviews productive, creative, and stimulating is to let the energy flow both ways! Rather than sitting the employees down and saying, "Here's where you are goofing up and here's where you're doing good and here's where you're so-so," which is the old way of doing things, allow your employees to give feedback on their performance, and on the problems and challenges they face. Make the review a mutual discussion of the work performance.

Some of our best managers allow employees to review themselves prior to sitting down to their review with the manager. Generally, employees are much harsher on themselves than the manager will be. This can be a very helpful starting point for two-way communication.

Irrelevant Evaluations

The problem of relevance arises most often with large "corporate" review programs and programs that have been in place for a long time. Make sure the review has direct application to your daily work environment—tasks, customer services, coworker relations. Ideally, some task, some event or relationship in your employee's daily experience should remind her of what was said at her review every time she comes to work for at least the following week. Make the review practical, make it timely, make it useful.

Subjective Reviews

The issue of subjectivity or bias can be rectified only if you as a manager have input into the creation of the performance review. Most reviews are in fact quite subjective, but it seems apparent that the more we can quantify the review process, the cleaner and clearer the review is going to be. When it is more objective, the worker can perceive that the review isn't simply a matter of personalities, that there are indeed some fundamental job expectations that are being made and, we hope, met.

But how can you quantify these seemingly intangible matters? It's not that difficult. For instance, the answer to the question, "How well does the employee get along with her coworkers?" is often graded on a numerical scale (5 = very well, 1 = very poorly). But we can also be less subjective—and more helpful—by asking *how often* the employee volunteers assistance without being asked, *how often* the employee does things that make everybody's work easier, *how often* the employee is late, *how often* the employee takes over other shifts, *how often* the employee initiates humor. These criteria can be subjective, even though numerically answered (5 = often, 0 = never), but it gives the employee an idea of what it means to be helpful to coworkers.

You should always review your employee's file to see precisely what has happened since your last review. Look at all paperwork and reports prior to conducting your review to ensure that your evaluations encompass the entire spectrum of your employee's work.

Some Legal Concerns

It's fashionable for consultants and legal departments to stress the use of job evaluations as backup for potential problems with employees. For instance, if an employee is fired, and then brings suit for unfair practices, the job evaluation form that shows the employee to be a troublemaker or a shirker of duties will bolster the employer's case in court.

Although we recognize this as a necessary aspect of the performance evaluation, it is the least helpful use of the review and should be given minimal attention. For legal purposes, as well as for business efficiency, you need to be upfront and honest about the employee's work habits. You should never sugarcoat the report just to make the employee feel good. And yet the primary purpose of the evaluation should never be to cover yourself in case of a lawsuit. Rather, the evaluation should help your employee fit in better and make her job experience more productive.

Thus, the purpose of the performance evaluation is to help both the employee and the manager improve service, productivity, and communication. It serves as a legal backup only after these functions are fulfilled. If an employee is, in fact, in danger of being fired for poor work performance, this should be made clear in writing, with details and ways to improve and with specific time lines indicated. Then, progress reports documenting either failure or success in meeting the time lines should be shared with the employee and included in the personnel file. Such reports will easily counterbalance previous "passing" or positive evaluations that might have been given.

Today's approach to hiring, especially regarding hourly employees, mandates that the employer operate with the assumption of honesty, integrity, and fair play on the part of all workers. And that if there is to be a parting of the ways, ninety-nine times out of a hundred it will be amicable. Is this naive? No. It's self-fulfilling!

Higher Productivity Comes With Happier Workers

In the past fifty years, a vast amount of research combined with cross-cultural practical experience has proved that you get what you focus on, as an individual, a company, or a country. If you focus on mistakes, you get mistakes. If you focus on solutions, you get solutions. It's a simple, but very powerful truism.

In the past, most work performance evaluations were focused on increasing productivity. It was assumed that the way to do this was to "help" employees see where improvements could be made. But if increased productivity is the intent of all evaluations, then no matter how productive the employee already is, he will always be encouraged to increase productivity. This is like the old *Candid Camera* skit in which pies come down the conveyor belt at a rapid clip, and no matter how fast the worker works, she can never catch all the pies because the line is always speeding up.

If a manager is only interested in higher productivity, she will always find reason to criticize and diminish a worker's input, even if she couches her criticism in the most friendly and helpful ways. On the other hand, if the manager is looking for ways to make the job more enjoyable, these evaluations become dynamic, exciting "think sessions" from which everybody benefits. And as you might guess, higher productivity is the natural by-product of a happy worker.

As your employees go through more and more reviews where it is clear that you are focusing on what helps your employees to enjoy their work, they will start looking forward to these reviews, and start taking them much more seriously. Why? Because they love to talk seriously about what makes them happy. The intent is to create a new workplace environment where everybody works well together, easily, openly, creatively. To achieve this new workplace environment, communication has to flow effortlessly in all directions. In Steve's company, like most other companies, he has customer comment cards to obtain feedback on products and services, and he uses the information gained from them as part of his review process. He also employs secret shoppers, who monitor his stores with random visits. Both of these customer evaluations are used when the manager sits down to talk with individual employees about their work.

But he takes it both ways. This is also the time that he gets feedback from the employees as to how they are feeling about the customers and about the company's secret observers. Is there some unworkable policy or rule that makes secret shoppers an uncomfortable possibility? Why? This is a good time to put the cards on the table. It's a time for two-way communication.

Likewise, every six months you should give your employees an opportunity to review their managers, their stores, and their overall success with the company. Try not to ask for these reviews at the same time you are doing your review of employees, though in both instances the two-way feedback is important. When you ask your employees to evaluate you and your company, you will receive many valuable comments, suggestions, and insights that will increase your profitability.

It's also important to conduct "corporate" reviews with your bosses and managers, asking for their feedback on your general operations. At every level, continually work to improve these evaluations and make them more practical. You "evaluate your evaluations" to ensure that you are staying up-to-date and focused on your primary concerns.

Remember the story in Chapter 4 about the employees who were playing hooky by going across the street to the bowling alley? If the bowlers were not keeping score, or they could not see how well they were hitting the pins, how long would their interest last? That's why evaluations are so important. Players like to keep score and they want to see how well they're hitting the pins. If you're not having fun with your evaluations, it's time to begin.

★ ★ ★ ★ ★

A well-kept evaluation program is one aspect of an overall environment that keeps your employees interested and "hooked" on your business dream. With that said, let's admit that sometimes it gets to a point where you no longer *want* to retain a particular employee—enough's enough and you've had enough! So what do you do in a situation like this? We get fired up about exactly this topic in the next chapter.

13

Boss, Won't You Please Fire Me?

We make our own fortunes, and call them fate.
—Benjamin Disraeli

Sometimes it's only right to fire the slob, the jerk, the slacker—
you know whom we're talking about. He's obvious, she's obvious,
everybody agrees: This one's not working out. The only question
is when, where, and maybe how to give him or her the ax.

And then there are the other times when you secretly wonder if perhaps you need to fire some guy who's been with you a
long time, who maybe helped you out when you really needed
help, and whom you couldn't have gotten along without, back
then. But now something's happened. Things have changed, and
he's just pulling you and everybody else down. Nothing you've
tried seems to work—and you've tried a lot of things. Your patience has run thin. He may have a great gift for gab, but you're
not communicating well with each other. Do you fire him?
Agony and heartache accompany this one. You feel a lot of maybe's and maybe not's.

The Tough Call

Let's talk about the tough one first: the employee who is a question mark. This is the "maybe I should and maybe I shouldn't"
situation.

Experience shows that if you're agonizing over whether or

not to keep an employee, nine times out of ten it's best to let him go. We're assuming here that you have already gone through several evaluations, the "hard talks," the "What can I do to help you improve?" conversations. For legal purposes, you've communicated in writing several times both your dissatisfaction and your expectations. But things have not improved, at least not much. And now you're tired of the problem. You'd like to just fire the guy.

Here's a tip: Do it! After all, this really isn't a marriage. At bottom, this is *not* a family relationship. It's not a guru-devotee agreement that demands forgiving "seventy times seven." This relationship involves not only you, the manager, and your employee, but also your customers and your business. So when you find yourself agonizing over whether or not to fire an employee, it's best to go ahead and let him go.

You never agonize alone. If you're feeling the agony, chances are good that the employee is also having the agony ("Should I stay or quit?"). And so are his coworkers ("Either they fire that guy pretty soon, or I'm out of here"). And, most of all, your customers are probably (quietly) agonizing ("Why in the world would they keep someone like that?"). Remember, you never agonize over a happy, effective, efficient worker. And that's whom you want to work with. That's whom you deserve to work with, and so does everybody else.

When you're agonizing over an employee, even if you don't say anything, everybody can feel it and it erodes confidence, compatibility, and business culture. Many times over the years, we've agonized over firing somebody, and sometimes held off and sometimes didn't. And when we've held off, we've almost always ended up firing the person later. We've never regretted a decision to fire somebody. It's always turned out best for all concerned.

We have, however, sometimes regretted the manner in which we have fired people. We recognize those circumstances where we could have been more compassionate, more understanding, perhaps softer and quicker, and thereby made it less painful for everybody. And we've gotten better about this action—wiser, over the years. But we have never wished that we had made a different decision.

Remember, this is not a boyfriend or girlfriend, husband or wife, splitting up, where years later you still may have doubts as to whether you did the right thing, even though, as a manager with an unhappy employee, it may feel this deep.

There are also times when the firing decision is obvious, and there's no agonizing over what to do. The decision to fire somebody is made easier if you internally review whether you have done everything you could to help the person improve. Was this person aware of your expectations? Did this person know what you wanted done? Has he been shown how to do it? If the answers to these questions are yes, and the person is still not performing well, then it is the worker who has created this situation and not you. It's your responsibility to handle the situation, even though you didn't create it.

Naturally, as with all managers and business owners, you will have many employees who come to work for you for a season or two and then, on their own, decide they need to go elsewhere. You will often wish you had these people back. You will indeed regret their leaving. But with such employees you'll always part amicably, wishing each other the best. Many will come back around to say hello. And you'll only half-jokingly try to hire them back. This is clearly a different scenario. We say this especially for the younger managers who are struggling with the problem right now. Go ahead, do what you're thinking about doing. It'll just make everything easier for everybody after you've done it!

How to and How *Not* to Fire People

Let's start with the hard part: how *not* to fire an employee. Here are ten ways *not* to give the ax to your worker:

1. *Don't fire someone when you are angry.* Deal with the situation instead. Take care of the employee's latest goof, or the fact that she called in sick, or that she broke the wheel. When you're angry you may indeed think, "This is it; this is the last straw." But wait until you've cooled down.

After the adrenaline rush, if you still feel that it was the last straw, then go ahead and do it. If you wait until you cool down, your coworkers will respect you more, your employee will handle it better, and you will feel better about it, too.

2. *Don't do it in front of everybody else.* Word will get out to the other employees soon enough. You don't want to make an example this way. Keep your cool, keep your respect by doing it in private.

3. *Don't try to justify your decision or argue about it.* When you're firing someone, it's not the time to try to correct the person or justify yourself. You'll read more about this in the next section.

4. *Don't warn the employee.* We assume you've already talked with your employee numerous times about changing his ways or improving performance. You've told him what needs to be done, what needs improvement. If you're down to firing time, it's no time for warnings like, "Bob, I'll want to see you in my office next Friday." It's always, "Bob, I need to see you NOW."

5. *Don't give notice of firing.* Don't give a week's notice, even a day's notice. This shouldn't need to be said, but I've seen firing done this way with disastrous results. When you let somebody go, let the person go right now.

6. *Don't fire someone because of age, sex, race, or religion.* Do we need to say this? Of course not. This is the end of the twentieth century.

7. *Don't bargain with the employee.* It's too late to bargain. You don't want to say, "If you come in on time for the next two weeks, you can keep your job." Or, "If you learn to treat the customers better, you can stay." Being threatened with job loss is the least motivating, least effective way to keep and train employees. This is always understood: If employees don't do right, they don't keep the job. No sense in drawing it out.

8. *Don't fire employees over the phone.* This is often a temptation, but you should resist that temptation. Believe it or not, it doesn't make it easier, and almost always makes it harder on both you and the employee. You have to do it face to face. In the next section, you'll see how to make such encounters nonconfrontational.

9. *Don't fire based on somebody else's word alone.* When there has been a problem of employee theft or abandonment of duties, and one employee snitches on another, it's tempting to reach a hasty conclusion. You may have suspected it all along, but for legal protection you need more proof than just one person's word. Make sure you have your facts, documented.

10. *Don't shift responsibility for firing to "corporate."* If you're not confident in your reasons for firing the employee, then maybe you shouldn't do it yet. Blaming the firing on a new corporate shakedown robs both you and your employee of the truth. What feels like a short-term gain ("I don't have to take responsibility for this") turns quickly into a long-term loss. Employees talk to each other. Secrets don't remain secret very long. Make it clean, make it honest, and everybody comes out ahead.

Make the Firing Go Smoothly

The assumption is that before things came to this point, you hired as best as you could, and that you trained as well as you could, and that you communicated, and had others communicate, many times in many ways. Presumably, you used your evaluation process to wake up the employee to your own expectations and his place in meeting those expectations. We assume that you clearly communicated when these expectations were not being met, and explained what he could do in order to meet them. In other words, you tried everything you could try to bring the employee along, and that nothing you tried worked.

So obviously this employee is not happy working for you. And the feeling is apparently mutual. It's time to call it quits. Learn to do it quickly, cleanly, without recrimination. Though firing someone you've selected and trained for a job can be difficult for you, the experience isn't pleasant for the employee, either. It can indicate failure on his part, and no one likes to think of himself as having failed. Of course, not all firings are like this, and often the employee is just begging to be let go (more about this later in the chapter). But whatever the circumstances, you want this break to be as comfortable as possible for both parties.

Take Time to Select the Right Time

Every business has its own time patterns, and only someone familiar with those patterns can decide the best time to let someone go. In traditional nine-to-five corporate America, it's generally agreed that the best time to let someone go is late on Friday afternoon. This gives the former employee the weekend to "settle down," and keeps other staff members from getting together to talk about it, either complaining or gloating. And Mondays are traditional days to start new, so you're not clouding a week.

Obviously, if you are firing somebody for stealing, or for drunkenness or some other unpleasant incident, then time is determined by the infraction. But if the reason is an accumulating series of incidents, then it is best to choose a time when it will have the least effect on the rest of the crew. For many restaurants, this is Monday morning, after the weekend rush. Or in retail, it may be after the rush surrounding the spring sale. For quick-serve gasoline stations, it might be after a holiday rush.

Yes, it is OK, generally, to pick a day that is best for you, when your own labor needs are not so immediate. Is this fair? Yes and no. Apparently the employee is not giving his best. You need to do what's best for you and the company. Just don't wait until the spring thaw.

Do It in Private

Being let go is most often an embarrassing, sometimes humiliating and self-demoting experience. No one likes to go through such an experience with an audience.

Some managers worry about violence from an employee, and if this is a pattern in the past, then you may need to have someone else with you for backup. Preferably this will be someone higher in the organization, rather than a coworker or an assistant manager. The chances for violence actually increase when the firing is not done in private because, in front of others, the worker may feel more inclined to defend his honor and pride.

If you follow these tips for firing, you won't be offending

anyone, and shouldn't run into "hurt pride," at least on the surface. The exception to this is when there appear to be potential legal problems with the employee (such as unlawful termination or discrimination) and you want to have a witness. Generally this witness is silent. It's a heavy role to play. Johnny the stock clerk may not be up to it.

Be Clear, Quick, and Certain

Don't beat around the bush. At a firing interview, you should open the conversation right away with the bad news. "John, I'm sorry to have to tell you that I've decided to let you go." Or "Mary, I've been agonizing over this decision but I've come to the conclusion I need to let you go."

It's only human to apologize briefly, though some consultants say it's not appropriate. Apologizing comes naturally, and so we do it—but only briefly and only when it's very clear that the decision has already been made.

Don't Argue

The time of firing is not the time or the place to be arguing the merits or demerits of the employee's performance. Such arguments have been made already, in previous encounters. This is not the place for discussion of job performance. The decision has been made. You have the authority to make it. You are exercising that authority.

To enhance that authority, especially for the termination of higher-level or longer-term employees, you may want to have a written statement of the reasons for termination available at the termination interview. Occasionally, you may want to have the employee sign the prepared statement, not necessarily agreeing with the reasons for termination but acknowledging that she is aware that these are the reasons given for the termination. A prepared statement of reasons for termination will most often immediately short-circuit the employee's temptation to argue, seeing that termination is a done deal.

Provide the Employee a Way to Save Face

Many young or inexperienced managers make firing a difficult process because they feel the employee needs to be told in no uncertain terms what he did wrong. We don't think that's necessary. In fact, we generally take the opposite approach. We admit that we really like the employee and are sorry that this situation didn't work out, that we're sure he will find someplace perfectly suited to his talents.

After telling the employee that we've decided to let him go, we generally say something like, "It's clear you're not happy here. Maybe you're too talented in other directions and so maybe that's why you haven't been as interested in this work." If you think about it ahead of time, you can come up with good ways for your employee to save face. "This is clearly not a job you like." Or, "You obviously have talents that aren't being used here." Or, "You're looking for opportunities that we're simply not able to give you."

The very fact that your employee is now being fired demonstrates that you are the boss, and that there is no question as to who has won the final argument. There's no need to argue any more. Let the employee think what he wants to think, this one last time. Remember, basically you want to make this a quick, clean affair, with the end result of getting the employee out the door. Don't let your own ego get involved.

Settle the Money Matters on the Spot

When possible (and in some states, by law) give the employee her final paycheck at the time of firing. This is part of making it quick and easy. You don't want the person coming back in for her check, and you don't want to have to think about sending it out.

Give the Employee the Benefit of the Doubt

When figuring the final paycheck, figure the total in the employee's favor. This also makes the parting easier for both of you. If there's a question on hours, overtime, or bonuses due, this isn't the place to pinch pennies. You don't want to reward the employee for poor performance or pay more than is coming, but you do want to make sure there are no questions about what is fair.

Especially for the employee who has been with you for a while but is no longer working out, a generous calculation on the final paycheck helps balance the relationship.

Collect the Company Property

Ask for return of company keys, uniforms, or tools right then and there, as you are issuing the final paycheck but before the employee actually receives the check. This is an awkward moment, and it helps to have a script in your head, if not actually written out. "If you want to get me your keys, I'll get you your check."

The best time to recover company property is after you have allowed the employee to save face. Where possible, make the return of company items a nonevent, such as, "Oh, by the way, let's bring in your tools." Loyalty and motivation are going to drop to absolute zero for most employees once they walk out with their final check, so it's best to clear the decks and have everything back in place before they take that walk.

Offer Reassurance

At the close of the firing interview, tell the employee again that you like him as a person and that you are sorry this didn't work out, and say how confident you are that there's a right job for him someplace else. This is only good manners and human compassion. People remember being fired many decades later. Make it as easy on them as you can. It is just as important to put your best face forward in the firing interview as it is in the hiring interview. Be professional. Be civil. Be human.

Don't Speak Ill of Those Who Have Gone

After the employee has gone, speak as highly as you can or as little as you can about the person to your current employees.

Most of the time, when you fire an employee the rest of the crew is relieved—happy to see them go. Even though it's tempting, this is *not* the time to join in their merriment, their jokes, and their snide comments about the departed employee. "He gave it his best shot. I appreciate him for it," is your more mature response. If you can't think of a good thing to say, it's best not to say anything at all—something like, "I'm glad it's over. I don't even want to think about it anymore."

This is a good time to earn a little genuine respect and solidarity with your crew by *not* bad-mouthing the departed employee. It's a good time to say, "I sure appreciate you guys, and what you're doing." Whenever you're tempted to talk about the departed employee, use that moment to instead encourage and reconfirm your faith in your current crew. They'll get the message.

Steve sometimes recommends to his managers that they prepare a simple statement about "why Bob is no longer with us." For legal purposes such a statement has to be clean and straightforward, and so such a statement may not be efficient in every case. But assumptions about why Bob was fired—especially if Bob had been with the company a long time or if there were criminal activities or other mysteries involved—can turn into rumors that may erode employee confidence. You don't want employees to think you're hiding anything. "Bob was let go according to company policy regarding. . . ."

A word of caution: In some states, it's illegal to tell the rest of the company what an employee did wrong, even if what you say is true. Be careful here. Know the law in your state before issuing any statements. Simply make it as civil as possible, as clean as possible, and then move on. That's the "moral law."

Boss, Won't You Please Fire Me?

Firing someone is oftentimes the best thing you can do, not only for the company and its customers, and not only for the remaining crew, but also for the disenchanted worker. When a square peg is in a round hole, nobody's happy.

People often feel hurt and insulted and strained when they

get fired. But once it's done, the person who has been fired often feels relieved, freed, ready to start again. Sticking with your joy, you'll know when and where and how to let someone go. And you'll do it more deftly, with grace and compassion. And you'll quickly recover, and move on. And so will they.

Close to the dawn of a new millennium, we're all learning to find the work that suits us best, to follow our hearts and our highest ideals. And simultaneously we're learning to let go of that work in which we have found no joy, no passion, no humor. As managers, it's our job to reveal this joy, this passion and humor, to those we manage. And it is just as much our job to release those who, for reasons of their own, are not yet able to respond to our priorities.

Sticking with your joy, you'll know when and where and how to let someone go. And, more important, sticking with your joy, the occasion will come up less and less for you as the years go by!

★   ★   ★   ★   ★

In the concluding chapter, we'll quickly review where we've been, where we are, and where we are going. And then you can get back to the delightful work of solving your hiring crunch.

14

Just Tell Me What You Want: An Opinion Survey of Workers

The perception of a problem is always relative. Your headache feels terrific to the druggist.

—Ramona E. F. Arnett

Wouldn't it be nice to know what *really* matters to today's employees? What are their priorities? What motivates them? What makes them choose one job over another?

To both prepare this book and quicken our professional growth as managers, we decided to invest a couple of thousand dollars in conducting an informal survey of entry-wage workers in our region—people who work in restaurants, retail outlets, quick-service gas stations, and the like. It turned out to be a lot of fun, with some surprising and some not-so-surprising results.

We recognize that if we had wanted to make our survey scientifically valid, we would have had professionals put together precisely worded questions and use double-blind tests and counterbalancing input paradigms to come up with statistically valid duplicative results. Professionals would have told us that we can't just have people bring in their survey for a free sub—which is what we did—and have statistically sound results. And, in fact, we did have one survey returned in a sealed envelope with only a single line filled in. The line said, "I turned this in because I really needed the sandwich. I just got fired. Thanks."

So it cost us a sandwich. But we had over 250 other respondents, from all ages, in many industries, tell about their experiences. And we learned a great deal about exactly what we wanted to know. We read, in these workers' own handwriting, what they were thinking about in the areas that mattered most to us. Although you don't need to spend a couple of thousand dollars or take a survey, it will be helpful in meeting your hiring needs to find out what the entry-wage workers in your area are thinking and feeling about their jobs. Find as many ways as you can to get information. There's no such thing as too much input in the area of worker attitudes.

The following are the results of our survey.

How Long Do You Stay at a Job?

The first few questions in the survey were basic items asking the name of the respondent's current employer, the length of time working there, and how many other jobs in the same or similar industry the person had held. We then asked about the average length of tenure at these jobs.

The average length of stay for all respondents (all ages, all industries) was a little less than ten months per job! As might be expected, for youngest workers the length of stay was shorter and for older workers the length of stay was longer.

In all ages, and in every industry, however, almost all respondents tended to exaggerate their own length of stay (as determined by answers to previous and later questions). It doesn't appear as though anybody is especially proud of having three or four jobs in the last two or three years.

Conclusion: If you're experiencing a big turnover, don't feel as if your situation is unusual. Almost all businesses are experiencing steady turnover. A more subtle point is that the vast majority of workers still do want to be loyal—or at least appear to be loyal. They want to find a place where they can hang their hats for a while. Otherwise they would not be exaggerating their lengths of stay. It's simply *not* true that there's no loyalty these days.

Why Do You Like Your Job?

The next question we asked was which of their previous jobs they had liked the most, and why.

All of the respondents consistently said they had liked their jobs because, to quote a twenty-two-year-old, "the people, and the place, and the atmosphere was great."

Here's a sampling of responses for liking the job:

* The teamwork was great.
* There was no guessing. You knew exactly what you were supposed to do. And the people were for the most part great.
* Good money and a casual atmosphere.
* They were detail oriented. Customers and clients were great.
* I was my own boss. I was appreciated for the job I was doing.
* They gave me responsibility.
* I felt appreciated and part of the team.
* Excellent hours and flexible schedule.
* They don't kill you and work you sixty hours a week.
* Great management and teamwork.
* They treated me as a mature individual.
* The people worked hard and played hard.
* Good hours, good pay, good company.
* It was fun, and we got to listen to great music.
* I enjoyed helping people and taking the challenge of making a profit.
* The owners and managers were great.
* People, money, atmosphere.
* Managers weren't harsh.
* Great boss, great customers, wore whatever I wanted, good money.
* I was treated like family.
* It was privately owned, with room to grow. Good social environment, positive reinforcement, management ownership, down-to-earth.
* Traveled, met people, good money, fun coworkers.

* I was allowed to be creative. Had a good work crew. And I could set my own hours.
* I had my own space.
* Teamwork among employees in every department.

You get the drift. No surprises here, except maybe how seldom money is mentioned. When money was mentioned, it was consistently mentioned in conjunction with good atmosphere, good management, freedom, and respect. Money was mentioned less than 10 percent of the time, but it wasn't the most common and it wasn't the most important factor in what constitutes a good job.

Employees said they had a good job when people treated them well, when they were respected, when they were given a certain amount of flexibility, when the whole crew was hard working. Having a good job means working with a group of friends who share the work load.

Conclusion: This is exactly what we've been talking about. Is such a work space so hard to create? In order to have a good job, these workers said, management has to be friendly, warm, considerate—all of which come naturally when you are simply enjoying yourself and enjoying the others around you.

What Makes a Crummy Job?

As with what makes a good job, there were no real surprises concerning the opposite situation, though it was nice to see it in writing as to why these workers did not like their previous jobs. As one seventeen-year-old described her job in a shoe store, "The people were cold and I was not properly trained."

Other responses were:

* Too corporate (hotel chain).
* I couldn't stand the other employees.
* I was lowest on the totem pole for too long.
* Bad hours, bad pay, bad company.
* It was groveling work, hard stuff (country club).
* Low wages, bad hours, nasty coworkers.

* Corporate policies.
* Pay was bad. Managers were terrible.
* Poor treatment of employees. No appreciation for a job well done.
* No money in it.
* Long hours.
* It was like working in a Nazi prison camp.
* Corporate-run businesses are tightwads.
* Corporate America, treated like a number; nonpractical and egotistical management.
* Weren't allowed sufficient break time. Understaffed for amount of business.
* Too businesslike in every aspect; employee conduct and counting every piece of wasted food.
* Management was too power happy.
* Management was terrible.
* Low wages, bad work conditions, nonenjoyable work atmosphere.
* Boring, not very challenging.
* Worked in (retail department) alone, and I like to work with people.
* No one ever asked me how I feel and no one cares that I worked too hard or that I carried so many other people's loads.
* Other people's loads, and low pay.

It seemed that if somebody didn't like the job, then the poor pay was more likely to be mentioned. Poor pay was mentioned three times as often in describing the poor jobs as it was in describing the good jobs. But on average, the pay was probably the same.

Conclusion: Poor pay becomes a factor when all the other factors of a good job are absent. If your boss is crummy, you're a lot more likely to scrutinize and evaluate your paycheck! More about this in a minute.

Before we go any further, it's only fair to mention that many questionnaires came back blank for this question or were marked N/A, not applicable. "I've liked all my jobs" was written on many of the surveys. Others simply didn't bother to answer the question.

Another consistent factor was that the respondents spent a lot less time talking about the crummy jobs. When we asked why they didn't like the jobs, the answers were consistently one or two or three words long, as compared to paragraphs about why they liked their jobs. This proves the point that people naturally want to enjoy themselves and thinking about jobs they do not enjoy is going to elicit fewer responses.

It was interesting how often respondents said that they didn't like working at a particular place because it was "too corporate" or "too businesslike." At the same time, they responded earlier that they had liked working with high-quality coworkers and organized management, where attention to detail was given high priority—all of which are equivalent to being "corporate" or "businesslike." What was the difference?

Here's a theory: The negative connotations of "corporate" and "businesslike" have come about because we've all seen so much television and watched so many movies where businesspeople and corporate types are portrayed as working without joy and without regard for other people's feelings ("Nobody ever asked me how I feel!").

When our respondents said they didn't like their jobs because things were "too corporate" or "too businesslike," the physical work circumstances were similar to other jobs that they reported enjoying. So the principle is again demonstrated: A good job is not so much what you're doing but the joy you have in doing it, not only for yourself but also for those who work with you.

If a manager is not having fun, is not enjoying his work, then he appears "corporate" or businesslike. Poor managers pick out one or two coworkers they enjoy and consider the rest of the workers "outsiders" (outside the manager's joy) assigned to the "slave jobs" and the dirty work. In such an atmosphere, the pay is "too low." When people aren't enjoying themselves, you have to pay them at least twice as much, and still they won't think they are being paid enough! In contrast, good managers consciously enjoy relating to *all* the people they are managing. Joy is an essential company benefit!

Why Did You Choose Your Current Job?

There was a surprising consistency in the answers to this question. What was surprising is how often these people chose their job "because it was close to home." In Chapter 8, we discussed different ways to attract employees other than classified ads. You can see why we gave special credence to the idea of flyers and doorhangers distributed in the neighborhoods surrounding your business establishment. Judging from the responses, having a job close to home is *very* important for entry-level workers.

We had assumed that people were choosing their jobs based on the reputation of the company, the management, or advancement potential—or at least the type of business. But no. "Where you located, man? I might come to work for you." Hrrmph. It makes a CEO shake his head.

Here are some of the other responses:

* I needed a job. Saw the sign.
* They gave me a choice of hours.
* I needed full-time work on the weekends.
* They worked with me on my school hours.
* They could give me full-time hours.
* Peeple. (sic)
* I needed a job.
* Wanted a job in retail.
* Reputation and availability.
* Good hours, good pay, good company.
* Because the people are great.
* Similar to what I was doing in my last job.
* Referred by a friend.
* I wanted cashier experience.
* Good reputation.
* Fun atmosphere.
* Works good with my schedule.
* Money.
* Because it is a nice store.

"Flexibility of hours" was often mentioned as the reason someone chose a job. Because of these comments, we've focused on this benefit as a bigger part of our classified ad campaign. Flexibility is not always an easy benefit to offer, but is something that is profitably developed whenever possible.

Location and flexibility of hours were the two most common reasons given for choosing a job, and from there we had a whole raft of different responses, as indicated above. "I was referred here" was a fairly common response, as were "reputation of the company" and "fun atmosphere." Money was mentioned fairly often, "high pay" hardly at all. We can assume that people would not be working unless they were in need of money, so that's why they chose the job.

Conclusion: What might be as important in this question as the answers we received are the answers that we didn't receive! One woman mentioned she wanted to gain "cashier experience," but she was a lone voice. All the rest of the respondents consistently neglected mentioning any interest in learning the trade. We read this to mean that people are not taking entry-level positions with a view to advancing in that industry.

Of course, as we all know, many of us end up making careers out of jobs that we took on the way to somewhere else. So maybe it's not surprising that so few people in this survey saw their current jobs as first steps to bigger and better things. Most of them saw their jobs as fill-ins while they were going to school, or until their husband got rich, or until they won the lottery. The absence of interest in learning the trade helped us refocus and downplay parts of our classified advertisements. We may love our industry and the potential it represents, but the entry-level worker appears to be more short-sighted.

How Long Do You Plan to Stay?

To such a straightforward and obvious question, we received some straightforward, interesting, and somewhat surprising answers.

We were surprised at how many respondents were planning to stay only a short while. Of course, we knew that turnover was high and that the average stay for entry-level workers is short. What we hadn't realized was that this was *part of their plan!*

We had assumed, largely based on our exit interviews and first-hand experience, that most entry-level workers quit their jobs because they just didn't work out, they were offered a better job, or they encountered problems at home, school, or love life. But no. Short-term employment didn't just happen because "something came up," or because things had changed, but rather, it was planned for all along! We weren't exactly shocked at learning this. But knowing that these short-term plans are fairly common has helped us to better implement our "stay with us" programs. It's nice to know that people are planning to leave from the very first, and that it is our job not just to provide a good working environment but to get them to change their minds about leaving. That's a different level of "romancing" from just working to keep them happy.

Conclusion: To get employees to change their minds about quitting, you need to break through to their deeper interests. When we hire, as we all know, we often all pretend that it will be a long-lasting relationship, or at least five years. And yet both sides recognize it probably won't be. It's nice to know that employees have to be coaxed into changing their minds about quitting. Once you know what your challenge is, it's easier to meet it.

Why Would You Leave Your Current Job?

Not so many surprises here. Most of the answers could be summed up in the four words we received most often: "better job, more money." If there were surprises, it would be in how many respondents suggested that they would leave the job if they moved. The possibility of moving was surprisingly prevalent.

Here's a sample of responses to the question:

* I won't!
* If I got fired.
* My boss is a jerk.

* Burnout—stress.
* Benefits.
* To go back to school.
* No progress (position or financial).
* Time off for a while.
* Am leaving after graduation.
* Higher wage, more convenience.
* Not enough time.
* Bad training.
* Not much appreciation from supervisory staff.
* For a job that was more fulfilling.
* Career advancement.
* Career aspirations.
* Death.

Although at the outset we don't attract many entry-wage employees by offering them career advancement and opportunity, when they get on board this is indeed a possibility that comes up for them. Many employees see their jobs as stepping stones during their high school or college studies. And as we all know, the change that life offers at the time of graduation is indeed one that most often entails a change in jobs, and rightfully so.

But there are many college graduates who can't find anything in their field, who recognize that they enjoy managing a restaurant, like working retail, or want to keep a small shop running. They see that the money they could earn by sticking with the company is often more than the money they could earn as an entry-level worker in their field of study. This is what we all secretly hope for!

Conclusion: Let's admit that this is the exception rather than the rule, and we would be paddling upstream if we were to count on postgraduation workers. It's only right that these young people spread their wings in the direction of their presumed interest. When school is not a factor, however, you can double your efforts to show employees that progress and advancement in your company are not only possible but also profitable and enjoyable!

What Is Best and Worst About Your Current Job?

We gave respondents one and a half lines to answer this question. Many of them also wrote in the margins. They liked talking about their jobs. But one thirty-year-old waitress could have been speaking for everyone when she answered both questions with three words. What she liked best about the job was "people." What she liked least about the job was "being ignored."

Time and again, "people" were the best thing about the job. People enjoy being needed, being appreciated, being part of a team. People enjoy people. So how much does that cost?

Here are representative answers:

* The best is hours and coworkers. Worst is working nights.
* Best—people and a good learning environment. Worst—nighttime work.
* Very boring, but not bad pay.
* The best is how much fun we have. The worst is the hours.
* The best are the employees, and managers. The worst are drunk people.
* The best—my boss. The worst—commuting.
* Worst—I don't like my boss. The best—I like working with some of the employees.
* Worst—$1/2$ hour from home. The best—atmosphere.
* Good money, good management. The worst: High stress due to lots of business.
  Best—I love the people I work with. Worst—I don't have enough to do.
* Worst is customers and no free meals. Best is sitting down.
* Best is the friends I work with. Worst is the low pay. (Same establishment where "good pay" was cited as one of the best!)
* Everything is fun.
* The atmosphere is what is best. The money is what is worst.
* Best is coworkers and supervisors. Worst is customers who come in with a bad mood.

As you can see, we didn't really find much variation in the answers here. We had some people tell us everything was good, but we couldn't find a single response where everything was bad. Again, we consistently found that what was good about a job was the people, primarily coworkers and supervisors, but quite often also the customers.

Very rarely did anybody say that the best thing about the job was that "the money was good" and then just let it go at that. Many of the respondents did in fact mention the money as what was best about the job. This is not surprising. After all, to earn money is in fact why we accept entry-level jobs. But apparently most respondents felt compelled to add that the people were also important in making the job "good."

We were surprised at how many people stated that the worst thing about their jobs was the customers. As the video store employee in the movie *Clerks* said, "This job would be great if it weren't for the [bleeping] customers!"

Conclusion: Working is a way for us to engage in the wider processes of life. Workers enjoy their participation, their contributions, their places in the wider circle. Honor this "deeper reason" for working. And teach your people to enjoy your customers.

What Percent of Employees Work as Hard as They Should at Your Job?

We were curious about how these employees felt about the burden they shared with their coworkers. In this question we probably could have used a professional to help us get the real information, but let's look at the results we got.

Eighty percent of the respondents who had been at their jobs for ninety days or less said that their fellow employees were hard working. The majority of employees who had been at their jobs for longer than this felt strongly that fellow employees were *not* pulling their weight.

This indicates that our trained veterans often feel they have their work down pat and that anyone new is seen as less knowledgeable, less experienced, less trained, less helpful or able to pull equal weight, no matter how good their intentions.

On the other hand, new employees (first thirty to sixty days) saw any fellow employee with more experience as a "smart working," confident genius!

Conclusion: Our responses showed even more clearly how it is a manager's job to forge the old-timers and the new recruits into a working team, supporting and encouraging each other. It is clear that the manager is the person to bring both balance and progress to the working crew. Everybody works hard—naturally, spontaneously—when they are being upheld by the manager's gentle vision.

Would You Have Any Interest in Growing Within Your Current Company?

This question was direct and obvious, and 64 percent of the respondents said yes. The fact that this directly contradicted what they had said earlier didn't matter. We were just happy to hear it.

This percentage is a lot higher than we might have supposed. More than half of the respondents are willing to advance in the company—to make their job something more than a stepping stone, to change their plans about quitting if someone offered them something to titillate their talents.

Conclusion: Look around at your employees and say to yourself, "two out of three of these people might be willing to stay and advance in the company, if I just give them a chance." If you look at half of your employees as long-term potentials, which should be very realistic if you hire right, wouldn't you be treating *all* of your employees a lot better? This survey has helped us do that. We hope it helps you, too.

What Do You Think Is a Fair Hourly Wage for Performing Your Work: above average _____, average _____, below average _____

We had a wide range of responses to this question, with some people saying that "anything less than $10 an hour (working in a convenience store) was below average."(The same respondent also wrote, in the comments section, "I'm a sap and I get used like one! I don't feel that I am a vital or valued employee. I also get tired of having to go out into the snow to smoke!") Although we had exaggerated responses to what the jobs were worth, we were most struck by the timidity that most respondents showed in answering this question. Most respondents stayed very close—from 50 cents to $1.50—to the amount they were in fact already being paid.

Conclusion: Seeing this result, we recognized once again how close management and workers actually are when it comes to establishing fair pay. We are *not* antagonists in this department. We do understand each other! And we were pleased to see that most workers suggested that average pay was very close to what they were already receiving. For low pay, we consistently received "minimum wage" for an answer. The point we learned was that management and employees are *not* far apart when it comes to estimates about what is above-average, average, and below-average pay. Our pay scales are not out of whack!

Does Your Manager Treat You With Respect?

This question was a sophisticated, cleverly worded, sensitive psychological probe. We were heartened to discover that almost 90 percent of the respondents answered yes. We are, on the whole, treating each other with respect. This is contrary to what the media would suggest, especially in television and movie productions.

The answer to this and the previous question suggest that capitalism as we now practice it is *not* a degrading or demeaning system, at least from the workers' perspective. And that's the perspective that counts the most. Yes, we had a little over 10 percent of respondents who said they aren't respected. It's interesting to note that these 10 percent are working under the same managers as those who say they are treated with respect.

Nevertheless, it's worthwhile listening to the comments. Along with this question, we provided two blank lines to explain how the manager either treated the respondent with respect or not. Here's a sample of the no-respect answers:

* It doesn't seem like my opinion counts very much.
* The manager doesn't know who I am.
* Sometimes he takes time to help, sometimes he doesn't.
* Only one supervisor is really rude.
* They don't care when you have dedication. When the smallest mistake is made, you're in trouble.
* He is a sexist pig (regional manager).

Now to be fair, we should give nine times as many samples from the respects-me column. A large percentage of the yes responses had no comments written as to why the manager respects the person. But almost all no's had comments. Here are some samples from the yes pile:

* The managers are all very common. No corporate bull.
* They respect me by listening to my concerns, taking care to make sure we have the supplies to do a good job, and being courteous and upfront.
* He's first to compliment me on a job well done. First to explain anything I did wrong and is more worried about doing right next time than scalding me for doing wrong this time.
* He knows I'm a self-starter so he lets me figure things out for myself.
* Allows me to set my own hours. Is willing to explain how to do new tasks.
* They're friendly, honest, respectable.
* They make you do what you have to, but are not rude. They're very listening, understanding (with the exception of the regional manager: he's a sexist pig!).

Conclusion: It's heartening to see how little it actually takes to earn the respect of employees: a little consideration, everyday honesty, ordinary manners. And 90 percent of us are doing this now! (And we can be thankful to the other 10 percent—those managers who make the rest of us look so good.)

Assigning Numbers to the Attitudes

To conclude our survey we presented a grab bag of items we wanted to know about. We asked the workers to rate the importance of each item on a five-point scale, regarding how important the item was to them and then whether they were actually receiving it. We averaged the responses and here's how it looks:

	Currently Receiving	Importance to You
Manager attitude/style/personality	4.2	4.6
Praise in public/reprimand in private	3.8	4.1
Decent crew synergy/team spirit	3.8	4.1
Wages	3.5	4.5
Cleanliness of store	4.1	4.4
Length between raises	3.2	4.1
Your voice/opinion gets heard	3.7	4.4
Training in first 3–4 weeks	3.8	4.1
Evaluated regularly	3.7	4.0
Positive feedback	3.7	4.4
Convenience to home/school/job	4.0	4.3
Career path/longevity	2.9	3.4
Number of hours	3.8	4.3
Safety/security	4.2	4.2
Perks/free meals/paid vacations	4.0	4.2
Flexibility for hours worked	4.3	4.5
Uniforms/comfortable/stylish	3.9	4.2
High standards/expectations	4.1	4.2
Company brand/reputation	3.9	3.6
Overall enjoyment of job	4.0	4.6

There were many surprises in these findings, most of them pleasant and useful. First, we were surprised to see that wages, although important for these people, were in fact less important to them than their manager's attitude, style, and personality. This confirms what other national surveys have shown: Fair wages are only one of many factors necessary for overall enjoyment of the job.

We were pleasantly surprised to see that cleanliness of the store tied for third. And not so pleasantly surprised that company brand name and career path were of the least interest to the respondents.

Quite clearly, these findings support our thesis that it is joy—happiness—that is the essential ingredient for successful employment and successful management.

Enjoying the Job

People want to enjoy their jobs. This is basic to the worker of the late nineties and early twenty-first century. As managers, we teach employees to enjoy their jobs by suggesting different thoughts they can enjoy about the job every day, every week. That's how we manage. And that's how we succeed.

There is still room for improvement, still ways that managers can help their employees enjoy their jobs. That's what this book has basically been all about. A large part of enjoying your job is enjoying your crew—enjoying the synergy of the team. This is where you as the manager are especially helpful. You find the thoughts to enjoy thinking about every crew member.

This survey suggests that your employees want to feel good about their coworkers—it's important to them—and as a manager you probably don't help them do that as much as you might. The job begins with each of us enjoying our own work, enjoying our own responsibilities, our own place in life, past and future. This is the first principle: Enjoying your work is the most important thing for you and all those around you.

In following this principle, your numbers, your classified ads, and your employee training and evaluations become elements of your People Plan, naturally falling into place. Such efficient happiness in your job is exactly what you're shooting for at the dawn of a new century and millennium. We're all pioneers.

Suggested Reading

Blanchard, Kenneth, and Spencer Johnson. *The One-Minute Manager.* New York: William Morrow & Co., 1982.

Coupland, Douglas. *Generation X: Tales for an Accelerated Culture.* New York: St. Martin's Press, 1991.

Drucker, Peter. *Managing in a Time of Great Change.* New York: Dutton, 1995.

Dyer, Wayne. *Everyday Wisdom.* Los Angeles: Hay House, 1993.

———. *Pulling Your Own Strings.* San Francisco: HarperPaperback, 1994.

Geneen, Harold. *Managing.* New York: Doubleday, 1984.

Gilles, Jerry. *Moneylove.* New York: Warner, 1988.

Heider, John. *The Tao of Leadership.* New York: Bantam, 1985.

Linklater, Richard. *Slacker.* New York: St. Martin's Press, 1992.

Molloy, John T. *How to Work the Competition Into the Ground and Have Fun Doing It.* New York: Warner, 1987.

Myers, David G. *The Pursuit of Happiness.* New York: William Morrow & Co., 1992.

Rosenbluth, Hal, and Dianne McFerrin Peters. *The Customer Comes 2nd.* New York: William Morrow & Co., 1992.

Tulku, Tarthang. *Skillful Means Gentle Ways to Successful Work.* Berkeley, Calif.: Dharma Publishing, 1978.

Waitley, Dennis, and Reni L. Witt. *The Joy of Working.* New York: Ballantine, 1986.

Zigler, Zig. *See You at the Top.* Gretna, La.: Pelican Publishing, 1972.

Index

achievement, "Congratulations"
   campaign for local, 93
advertisements
   airplane, 92
   handling responses to, 91–92,
     99–106
   help wanted, *see* help wanted ads
   radio, 91
   television, 94, 97–98
aggression
   employee, 55–56
   social, 36
airplane advertisements, 92
alienation, 57–59
Almayrac, Christian, 26–34, 56, 129
anger, in firing process, 148–149
appointments, setting, 104
attitude surveys, 157–173

baby boomers, 11
bait and switch
   attractive interviewers in, 96
   and pay rate, 96
banners, recruitment, 92
Bed Bath and Beyond, 75
BeHappy game, 26–36, 56
   benefits of, 36
   and Law of Happiness, 27–28,
     54–55
   and Law of Joyous Action, 31–34
   and Law of Linkage, 28–29
   and Law of Spontaneity, 30–31
   teaching, 55–56
Blankenthorn, David, 50

Bob's Stores, 73
bonuses
   referral, 88
   retention, 41, 87–88
   signing, 87, 126
   for survey takers, 93–94
boredom, 2, 3
Boston Market, 4
breaks, in training process, 117–118,
   119
bribery, *see* bonuses
brochures
   for applicants outside company, 76
   for in-house recruiting, 84–85
buddy system, in training process,
   116, 119
budgets, 39–41
   and help wanted ads, 70, 84, 124
   and hiring strategy, 40
   and recruitment, 19, 40
Burger King, 2, 126
Burns, George, 127
business cards, recruitment, 81–83
buyer's remorse, 77

Career Track, 137–139
carnivals, in recruitment strategy, 93
Census Bureau, U.S., 3
Cicero, 9
Circle K, 2
classified ads, *see* help wanted ads
clergy, referrals from, 67
Clerks (videotape), 58
Colbert Stores, 75

177